THE HAPPY HUMAN PLAYBOOK

A PRACTICAL GUIDE TO HEALING BODY, MIND AND EMOTIONS WITH JOY AND PLEASURE

ANTONIA HALL

Second Edition

This publication is a creative work protected in full by all applicable copyright laws, as well as by misappropriation, trade secret, unfair competition, and other applicable laws. No part of this book may be reproduced or transmitted in any manner without written permission from New Ventures Press except in the case of brief quotations embodied in critical articles or reviews. All rights reserved.

The information, methods and techniques provided in this book are designed to provide helpful information to be used for self-improvement. This book is not meant to be used, nor should it be used to diagnose or treat any medical condition. None of the information in this book is intended to replace appropriate medical and/or psychological treatment. The publisher and author are not responsible for any specific physical or mental health needs that may require medical supervision and are not liable for any damages or negative consequences from any treatment, action, or application to any person reading or following the information in this book.

New Ventures Press

The Happy Human Playbook: A Practical Guide to Healing Body, Mind and Emotions With Joy and Pleasure, Second Edition

Copyright © 2024 Antonia Hall

Library of Congress Cataloging-in-Publication Data
Hall, Antonia.
Library of Congress Control Number: 2020918122
Paperback ISBN: 978-0-9970850-7-5
eBook ISBN: 978-0-9970850-5-1

Published in the United States of America

Praise for the book

"Hall offers a sprightly self-help guide that will entertain as it teaches, aimed at helping improve well-being through the art of play and pleasure. The book references the scientific alongside the imaginative, pairing the two nicely into one interesting text. Creative and playful prose dots the pages of this guide, perfectly in sync with the book's theme. Hall uses imaginative metaphors to bring her suggestions to life. Hall's willingness to address topics that many books shy away from is refreshing, and she offers readers functional advice that comes with a sparky edge. The hands-on activities are useful and highlight the book's main concepts, and Hall is careful to leave space for each reader to customize her advice."
-Publishers Weekly, Booklife Prize

"Fascinating, informative, exceptionally well written, organized and presented, "The Happy Human Playbook: A Practical Guide to Healing Body, Mind and Emotions With Joy and Pleasure" will hold a particular appeal to readers with an interest in adult human sexuality and sexual well-being. While highly recommended for community and academic library Self-Help/Self-Improvement collections for it message that healthy, simple, physical pleasures can be mentally and emotionally transformative, it should be noted for personal reading lists that "The Happy Human Playbook" is also available in a digital book format (Kindle, $7.99)."

-Midwest Book Review

"*The Happy Human Playbook: A Practical Guide to Healing Body, Mind and Emotions With Joy and Pleasure* by Antonia Hall is an amazing self-help guide to unplug and give yourself breathing space to experience full body and mind peacefulness. Antonia Hall's writing has a deeply personal tone that speaks to you, and you can think of her as an authentic life coach that guides you on the path of realistically improving your circumstances and trying to make the best version of who you are. At the same time, the information contained herein is evergreen and will always remain relevant. True to its title, *The Happy Human Playbook* is a must-read if you want to zero in on the areas of your wellness and learn how to off-load for a happier life."

-Readers' Favorite

"*The Happy Human Playbook: A Practical Guide to Healing Body, Mind and Emotions with Joy and Pleasure* is a playbook for finding real pleasure in your body, your surroundings and--semi-radically these days-- actually enjoying your own life. The guidebook is filled with deep wisdom, a sense of fun and lots of inviting exercises--all grounded in a real sense of what makes life truly worth living. Reading Antonia Hall's soothing and encouraging words is like a balm for the soul (and body too--see also: the chapter on great sex toys!) and a clear path to occupying your own body and life."

-Jill Hamilton, journalist for Cosmopolitan and Oprah Magazine

"If you want to live, like *really* live - a rich, sensuous, abundant life - this book is for you. Hall shows readers how to show up, be present, and connect the dots between heart and mind awareness to achieve a play and pleasure filled life. *The Happy Human Playbook* teaches kindness and self-compassion through a series of simple mindful practices, enabling readers to experience all the beauty their body and its existence in this world has to offer. You'll feel alive, energized, and want to dance after reading Hall's joyful guide to being human."
-Ryn Pfeuffer, journalist and author of
101 Ways to Rock Online Dating.

"It can be hard to believe in magic when you wake up every day in pain, thanks to chronic illness. Thankfully, Antonia Hall penned a book that reminds us that we're not alone, and perceived weaknesses can be our greatest strengths. This is a must-read for anyone in need of rituals and witchcraft to remind them of their power, as, after all, the most important ingredient in any spell is yourself."
- Sophie Saint Thomas, author of
Sex Witch: Magickal Spells for Love, Lust, and Self-Protection and *Finding Your Higher Self.*

Acknowledgements

This book could not exist without all of the Neuroscientists, Psychologists, and various Pleasure Pioneers who bravely paved the way for this work. Thank you to the Julia who provided the encouragement I needed to find my way to this book's completion. Endless gratitude to the Julia who always knows how to make my writings sing the right notes; you are such a gift. To Cathy and Beth for loving support and the best comic relief. In loving memory of Frank.

Contents

Introduction 1

Playbook Philosophy 1
How This Playbook Works 7
Playbook Truths 9
Stressed Vs Satisfied Test 10
My Relationship With This Material 11

Chapter One: Feet - Our Connection to the Material World 15

Creating a Personal Playground 16
Tuning In for Optimal Functioning 17
Admiring Natural Beauty 20
Grounding and Earthing 22
Letting Your Inner Child Pick a Pleasure 26

Chapter Two: Legs - How We Carry Ourselves 28

Choosing a Compost Pile 29
Returning to Who You Really Are 32
Shedding Body Shame 36
Lowering Energy: Finding Comfort with Stillness 44
Raising and Resonating Energy - Making Your
    Playbook Soundtracks 47
Dancing Your Way Through the World 50

**Chapter Three: Hips and Pelvis - Home of
Creativity, Angst and Orgasmic Possibilities** 52

Redefining 'Sex' and 'Orgasm' 53
Embracing Yourself as a Sexual Being 56
Understanding Your Sex Drive 58
Training Your Pelvic Floor 64
Making Peace With Self-Pleasuring 68
Getting to Know the Vagina and Vulva 70
Getting to Know the Penis 79

**Chapter Four: Abdomen - Where Emotions
Lurk and Power Awaits** 88

Engaging Energy-Body Awareness 89
Making Altars for Deeper Connections 91
Having Healthy Boundaries 93
Moving, Rocking, and Claiming Your Power 94
Showing Up for Your Life's Moments 98
Harnessing and Appreciating Life's Micro-
    Moments of Pleasure 101
Experiencing Appreciation Through your Senses 103
Connecting with Pleasure in Your Body 104
Exploring Your Erotic Pleasures 106
Shaking Your Hips and Booty 109
Picking Out a New Toy 110

**Chapter Five: Heart, Chest and Lungs -
Expand Here for Immense Healing** 115

Encouraging Self-compassion, Self-Acceptance,
    and Self-Love 116
Making a Heart-Mind Connection 119

Feeling the Love: Antonia's Rosewater Practice 124
Using Breath to De-stress and Heal 126

Chapter Six: Throat - Communication Center and Bridge to the Outside World 130

Nourishing Up 131
Reclaiming and Re-Awakening Your Taste Buds 133
Throwing a Feast in your Honor 135
Speaking With Intention 137
Exploring the Sounds of Your Pleasure 138

Chapter Seven: Head - Hub for Problems, Solutions and Experiences 143

Assessing Your Distractions 144
Bringing More Consciousness 150
Breathing Out of Overthinking..154
Singing Away Monkey Mind 155
Creating New Memories with Scents...............................155
Setting a Healthy Sleep Routine 159
Meditating Your Way Back to Yourself 161
Massaging in New Joys..164
Soothing the System with a Headrub 166
"Thinking" Your Way to Orgasm 168

Conclusion...171

Introduction

Playbook Philosophy

Simple pleasures and play have the power to change your life.

All are welcome, respected and will be referred to as "humans" throughout this book. Many of the practices detailed here are scientifically proven to contribute to your health and wellbeing, but they are often also forms of play. Isn't it funny how many of the activities we did as children are the very same practices scientific research and doctors are now recommending to help humans combat things like stress, anxiety, and aging, and to improve our health, happiness and sense of wellbeing? Some of the techniques in this book can lead to experiences of immense joy, and ecstasy. The desired result is to make your life feel as flowing, happy, healthy and pleasure-filled as possible.

Why do we need more pleasure? Unfortunately, we are a stressed out, anxious, and generally unfulfilled group of humans—not just in the western world, but globally. We are not enjoying basic pleasures. Uh, oh.

Be honest. Are you getting the most of your life experiences, or does true fulfillment feel out of reach? Here are some questions to assist you with assessing where more pleasure might enrich your life:

- How much of each day nourishes and enriches you?
- Do you enjoy the food you eat, and if you do is there any guilt later?
- Do the conversations and interactions you have throughout the day uplift you, or leave you feeling drained?
- Do you hope to experience sexual satisfaction or deepen your sexual pleasure?
- If you are partnered, has your sex life been leaving you feeling fulfilled or unsatisfied?
- When you worked your ass off for your last big winning accomplishment, did the accomplishment itself leave you feeling deeply fulfilled? Or did your last great win have you searching for outward validation to have it feel meaningful for you?

We weren't built for the world we have created for ourselves. There are too many things vying for our attention. The natural stress response wired to protect us from life's dangers is getting activated far too often.

Our ancestors saw a threat (oh, crap, a lion), registered it in the brain (fight or flight?) and the body responded (run, or kill-or-be-killed). This stress response is a product of neural pathways called the "autonomic nervous system" (ANS), divided into the sympathetic and parasympathetic nervous systems. Once the brain registers stress, the sympathetic nervous system produces a "fight or flight" stress response for self-preservation. This response gives the body a boost of energy, much like a gas pedal on a car, by releasing adrenaline and the stress hormone cortisol. The parasympathetic nervous system acts like the brake, allowing the body to rest and recover from the stressors.

Today we are inundated with what the body may interpret as threats, and the body's natural stress response gets frequently activated, which can become damaging to the body. Additionally, our body's response system is often unable to enact the action portion of completing that stress response. These stress responses need to get carried out, or they get stuck in the body, which can then pose more serious problems.

Imagine you are driving down the road and get cut off. Your impulse to react (swear, hit the horn, etc.) is your body's way of completing that stress response. If you meditate daily, live healthy, and haven't been experiencing many life stressors, your personal coping resilience is likely to be higher, and you may emotionally shrug it off. But if your daily life has been filled with pressures, long hours, and worries have kept you up at night, being cut off in traffic might elicit an intense experience of anger or even rage. All responses are a natural human response, but affected by outside sources and our reserves at the time.

The expression "built-up stress" is very real. It is one of the reasons that humans are using coping mechanisms to numb their bodies and minds. Unresolved emotional buildup in the body isn't comfortable. It can be an internal pressure cooker, waiting for opportunities for release. The desire to just make discomfort stop, even for a little while, is completely understandable.

Life can be overwhelming. Hitting the mute button can feel like a welcomed respite, but it does nothing to resolve the issue. Worse yet, numbing out the pain and frustration also numbs the ability to experience pleasure. Pleasure is naturally wired into our systems as a reward, as an antidote, allowing for the release of tension and stress in the body while also soothing and nourishing.

Here's a weird secret we don't get told often enough: healthy simple pleasures are good for you! For whatever reason, many of us live within structures that do not support exploration or discussion about pleasure, and this is particularly true about our sexual pleasure.

There are mountains of reliable, unbiased scientific data that unequivocally show us that when humans experience healthy pleasures, it greatly contributes to wellbeing physically, physiologically, psychologically, and relationally.

Enjoying sexual pleasure also has many health benefits and can contribute to our sense of overall wellbeing in remarkable ways. Cultural stigmas have created a lot of unfortunate narratives that keep us from enjoying pleasure in our bodies. When we start changing the flawed culturally prevalent stories around our bodies, sexuality and pleasure, it will make a positive contribution to each of our lives and have global benefits.

Our ancient ancestors relied on pleasure to guide them.

Today, we tend to lean towards seeing, inhabiting, and enjoying our bodies as a "guilty pleasure", or something we have to work really hard for all of our lives, instead of seeing it for what it really is: the healing balm that can leave us feeling fulfilled. This includes making peace with our intrinsic sexual nature. Sexual energy is one of the most potent resources we have access to, yet we rarely acknowledge, discuss, or utilize it.

Sexual pleasure was the energy that created you. Why do we never think of ourselves as the result of pleasure? None of us would exist without someone having orgasmed. We have all, quite literally, been orgasmically burst forth into being.

Your sexuality is another essential part of health and wellness. Sexual energy can be a special spark you can turn to as a powerful resource in your life.

Sexuality has become overly complicated. This playbook will help simplify things and offer ways to get past the biggest challenges humans tend to have around their sexuality.

Some of the most common sexual human concerns I hear include:

- Lack of sexual satisfaction and the inability to orgasm
- Trouble getting aroused
- Lack of desire and/or lack of interest in sex
- Body shame, feelings of guilt and sin around the body, pleasure, and/or sexuality
- Inability to get out of one's head, stay present and enjoy pleasure in the body
- Difficulty communicating about sexual wants and needs
- Faking orgasm
- Painful intercourse

Most cultures don't like to have conversations like these, but I enjoy looking at things from different perspectives, and the foundation for this is simple: many of us were not taught to enjoy our bodies, our human experience, and the simple pleasures all around us awaiting our attention.

This playbook is going to offer you ways to tap into basic human enjoyments, because simple pleasures are the answer many are seeking. We live in a world constantly vying for our attention, often leaving us feeling drained and unfulfilled. You will be reclaiming your body and your senses through this playbook, so you can experience the satisfaction you desire.

All are welcome here, and this playbook was designed to be used regardless of the type of human body you were born in, how you identify, or what type of sexual or romantic partnership you prefer. We are all human, and therefore all attendees are referred to as 'human'. I will clarify by using the terms 'humans with vulvas/vaginas', 'humans with clitorises' and 'humans with penises', when it is helpful for specific exercises.

Perhaps you already know many exercises in this book. You are likely doing some of them already. We hopefully all have a tool chest of wellness tricks we are utilizing. It is great if one of the simple pleasures is already a practice you use. When you come upon a technique with which you are familiar, greet it like an old friend.

If it is helpful for you to hear (because sometimes we need reminders): you have one hundred percent permission to enjoy your body. You have full permission to dive deep into this experience, enjoy the most you can from it, and to continue relishing every pleasure you can from your life.

You get one body in this lifetime. Were you taught not to love, trust, or even listen to it, as many of us were? As humans, we are commonly taught to carry shame and guilt around this one body we are given. Slapping labels like "sin" or "shame" on our bodies and our sexuality have done us zero favors. As though that wasn't enough, we are commonly given little to no guidance on how to enjoy these bodies, nor taught how very much pleasure we can experience in them!

Well, my Love, I am here to call BS on the negative messages we are taught to carry. No one has time for that anymore! It is time to love yourself, and the one amazing body you have been given. Make that body your friend. Because I am here to tell you that it is wired for such incredible amounts of pleasure. Love your body and it will love you back in magnificent ways!

Let's dive in, shall we?! Yes!

How This Playbook Works

Have you ever let yourself unplug and fully enjoy a moment of complete rest and relaxation? Perhaps you were on a dream vacation or relaxing in your own backyard. Maybe you let yourself unplug and find stillness on your couch on a lazy Sunday. For a beautiful space of time (minutes? days?) there was nothing you needed to do, and no other place you needed to be. Nothing pulled on your attention or needed you. You just relaxed, fully, and your body experienced peacefulness.

Ideally, you will give yourself a similar breath of space to fully be present with the practices detailed in this playbook. Each one is here to be of pleasure and value to you.

Show up. This playbook is for you. What brings you pleasure? You may choose to see this playbook as a big buffet of simple pleasures here for you to test out or rekindle in your life. Which pleasures do you most enjoy? Which are of the greatest benefit to your current lifestyle? Just rest into these exercises. See if they work for you. Do you derive pleasure from it? How's it feel? What happens when you try them? Be present for the techniques so they can be beneficial to you.

Presence. Oof. Let's be honest, we humans kind of suck at presence these days, despite its necessity. Do you want a life of fulfillment? Then you have to show up for it. Yep. The body has a reward system and we are reclaiming it. But you have to stay in the moment as much as possible. It'll be OK. There's lots of pleasure waiting for you.

With each practice you implement you are consciously rewiring your neurophysiological and neuropsychological systems so that your nervous system can calm down. This intentional reset is what you need to finally experience a true sense of satisfaction and happiness. It begins one simple pleasure at a time.

Be your own best, gentle, compassionate friend through this process. Taking time for this patient work pays off in a lifetime of real and true happiness. It isn't always easy. It is an ongoing process. Our society often teaches us to be unrealistic and hard on ourselves. We turn to others for validation rather than trusting our own innate wisdom. It can take time to wear away this programming. You deserve your own love and acceptance. Let these simple pleasures be your medicine, guiding you back to your own heart.

Playbook Truths

May these basic truths serve as a reminder throughout this journey:

1. Pleasure is your birthright.
2. Daily enjoyment of simple, nourishing pleasures in your body is a natural, positive way to contribute to your health, peace of mind, and happiness.
3. Respect is given to all, especially your beautiful self. We are all born worthy and deserving.
4. Your body is always communicating with you, and listening contributes to staying balanced, happy, and well.
5. Nature wired you with a desire for pleasure and a propensity for play and these serve as trusty guides towards that which is healthy for you.
6. Combining pleasure and play can naturally combat stress while bringing more joy and satisfaction to life.
7. You commit to your truest self by staying honest with yourself throughout this journey.
8. You must want to change for any real change to happen. All changes made are chosen and enacted upon by you, and you alone, and that is how miracles happen.
9. You will continually give yourself permission to be human, which means being gentle, loving, compassionate, and supportive of yourself. Real growth requires making some mistakes.
10. You know that with each new internal and external road you travel, you expand your consciousness and your horizons.

It might be helpful to use my Stressed Vs Satisfied Assessment throughout this playbook process. Just notice if you are experiencing more things listed in the first or second group of word listings.

Stressed Vs Satisfied Test

On a scale: Very often (4), frequently (3), sometimes (2), rarely (1), never (0)

In the last week, have often have you felt:

Tense
Over-extended
Too much on your mind
Not enough time for everything
Misfortunate or overly troubled
Anxious
Out of control
Not enough time to breath
Trapped
Wanting to give up

On a scale: Very often (4), frequently (3), sometimes (2), rarely (1), never (0)

In the last week, have often have you experienced:

Calm
In control
A sense of peace
Happy

Satisfied
Fulfilled
Grateful
Enjoyment
Lucky
Comfortable in your own skin

How to score your assessment test: Add each of the two totals. Ideally your second total will be substantially higher than the first number. This assessment is merely one tool to check in with yourself about how much nourishment your body, mind and emotions may be experiencing.

My Relationship With This Material

The exercises in this playbook saved my life.

For years I worked long hours and neglected my body. I was focused, driven, and work kept me in a headspace. Other distractions in my life, like social media and binge-watching, also kept my mind busy. While I tried to balance long work hours with exercise and time spent with friends, my life had become neglectful of real nourishment that could be derived from the many pleasures life offers us in this human experience.

The body can only be ignored for so long, and mine had taken the whispers of dissatisfaction to an epic level of discontent. I found myself spending a workweek in the hospital and learned that an autoimmune disorder was starting to cause issues. After three years and many healing modalities, but too few lifestyle changes, I learned that I was dangerously ill. I spent far too much time in bed, and with the lack of movement arthritis settled in everywhere. I continued implementing healing methods, but I was still spending too much of my time on work and distractions. I had forgotten that life is supposed to be fun.

With my blood tests getting more disconcerting, I decided to make my life as playful as possible. I dove headfirst into pleasure. I sang my way through tears and had "dance" jams from my couch. I implemented more techniques to turn inward, becoming a better observer of my mind and negative thinking patterns. Turning towards play brought the true fulfillment I inherently craved.

Some of the most beneficial practices I used were "sexual". When the pain was at its worst, I masturbated to give my body a natural dose of pain relief. Turns out those daily orgasms not only improved my mood, they boosted my immune system, and served as a pretty decent form of exercise I couldn't otherwise give my heart. I prioritized the messages my body had for me and made my life an exercise in balancing my inner drive and soul work with a committed exploration into the healthy pleasures life offers us all. My child-like enthusiasm for life offered my body the healthy physical, physiological, and psychological benefits it had craved.

The pleasure door gave me ways to turn things around and within months my doctors were baffled to find that my bloodwork was naturally returning to normal levels. Despite having become physically disabled, I had relearned how to really and truly enjoy life. By getting out of my head and into the present moment, I was able to build up pleasure wiring within my body. Through accepting my situation, I began a love affair with myself.

All of my efforts towards self-love hadn't really stuck until I learned compassion. By making time for, and befriending my body, becoming the observer of my mind, and wanting more for myself, I became the compassionate best friend my body, mind, and soul needed. This compassion and self-acceptance was the game changer. Acceptance evolved into real self-love.

Despite physical challenges, I not only derive pleasure from my life - I love life!

In fact, I have found that I seem to be having a lot more fun than most of the people I know.

I have seen how many humans struggle to find a way through the stress and overwhelm—chasing happiness, but unable to experience a real sense of fulfillment. I understood that feeling of discontent well, and I knew that I had to write a playbook of simple pleasures scientifically proven to change lives. I wanted to make this guide practical so it could be easily implemented by even the busiest of humans. I wanted to use language that would speak to as many people as possible.

This playbook for humans is the culmination of decades of study, research, and embodied wisdom. It took becoming seriously ill before I turned my stress, anxiety, and overwhelm around. Now I balance having fun with writing about ways for all of us to liberate our lives. The writing of this playbook was joyful, song and dance filled, and orgasmically birthed. It is as much a love letter to myself as it is to all of you. May it serve each of us well.

CHAPTER ONE

Feet - Our Connection to the Material World

Are you comfortable taking up space in the material world? From a young age we humans are usually directed in how to fit ourselves into the world around us. This world has expectations, set before our arrival. We won't all equally be greeted with the freedom to be comfortable taking up space.

As a female-identified human, I was taught by the society around me that my male-identified counterparts had more rights than I did to take up the space we mutually occupied. I spent over half a lifetime feeling squeezed and compressed. But learning to take up space changed my relationship with the material world around me. It began when I made more room for myself first.

I would like for you to make room for yourself in the form of a personal playground. Having a safe and comfortable place where you can have uninterrupted time for yourself is invaluable. Having an area or room where one can be alone makes life better for every human. Having a comfy private place to enjoy pleasure and play is going to feel wonderful. It will also be beneficial for many of the exercises in this book.

Creating a Personal Playground

If you don't already have one, you are going to be creating your own little nest where you can take time for yourself, chill, get cozy, muse, reflect, and enjoy delicious times. Mood makes a big difference, and the same principle applies for both solo time and partnered activities. Having some ambiance creates that soft, sensual bubble in which turning both inwards and towards pleasure and play is more inviting.

If you don't have the luxury of a room to yourself, having a few chosen items that can be brought out (and put away) can quickly transform a shared space or corner of a room. Much like a pop-up shop! But, your own special pleasure pop-up space.

Bring items in that will lend a sense of comfort, like a soft blanket and pillow. You may want fresh flowers, incense, candles, or a soft-lit lamp. Fabrics can quickly change the feel of a room or area. What will allow you to bring in the elements and qualities you desire? Just please be careful when mixing flowing fabrics with candle flames. Remember that the playground should have ample space to safely writhe in pleasure without threat of burning the house down.

I would recommend going into your intended chill space area and spending some time in it. Does it evoke the vibe you are envisioning? The playground can be as simple or elaborate as you want to make it.

Sit in your space. Lie down. Do you have enough pillows? An extra pillow or two come in handy in sensual spaces.

My most basic playgrounds usually include the addition of a soft blanket, a candle, and some form of scent (natural incense, room spray, etc). It only takes a few basics to transform a corner into my makeshift sexy time area. I have also used a sex blanket (made specifically to be waterproof, protective, and easy to wash) as one of my quick sexy space-creating tools. My insta-playground.

Make it fun. Make it simple, or make it a fantasy come true.

Tuning In for Optimal Functioning

Everyone from general medicine doctors to sex therapists to athletic coaches recommend body scans as a way to ease stress, reduce pain, and increase one's capacity for pleasure.

All you need is a brief focused amount of time in an uninterrupted space. Body scans are a quick way to check-in with your body. Over time they will become something you automatically do more often. Your body is speaking. It wants to be healthy and in balance. Are you listening?

Our human body has a natural rhythm and flow, just as all nature around us does. Through tuning inward and seeing where your physical body is out of alignment you can notice small imbalances and correct things before they become big imbalances. Touching base with your body is smart self-care that will leave you feeling better.

In the mornings, take a moment to turn inwards. Pay attention to your body and notice what feels stuck. The body wants to move. It wants to be flexible and flowing. When tuning into my body, I have found it helpful to ask, "How can I invite more fluidity and flow into my body?"

Body scans are a great way to open a dialogue with your body. I have found them to be integral to my own health and wellbeing. The more I tune into my body, the more I am able to hear what my body is needing and can address those needs before they become real issues. These regular check-ins will have you making friends with your body, which will support your pleasure and wellbeing for the rest of your life. Plus, body scans are a quick way to release stress, ease anxiety and bring more presence and awareness to the moment, all of which increases the body's potential for experiencing enjoyment.

Try the scan below at least once a day for the next week. Notice if this dialogue with your body leaves you feeling more relaxed and centered. After a week, make notes about the benefits of how checking in with your body has contributed to your week. Might daily body scans be a helpful tool to use each day?

Basic Body Scan

Close your eyes, and tune inward during a time when distractions are limited. You may do your scan sitting or lying down. Choose what works best for you.

Become aware of your body. Notice how your body is supported. Take three slow deep breaths.

With an easy inhale, notice as the air makes its way into your body, paying attention to the expansion in your lungs and chest. With each breath, allow a sense of deeper relaxation and ease into your body.

Feel the weight of your body and place your attention on your feet. Are they touching the floor, or relaxing as you lie down? Notice any pressure, heat, coolness, and other sensations.

Continue allowing your breath to flow in and out with ease.

Bring your attention up to your calves, knees, and then up to your thighs. Is there tension or tightness, or are they relaxed? Move up to your hips, stomach and when you are ready, your chest. Is there any pressure, stress, or other sensations your body would like you to pay attention to?

Bring your attention up to your shoulders, neck, and finally your face. Breathe in and as you exhale relax your jaw. Soften your facial expression.

Give your full body your attention. From your toes up to your head.

Just listen in. "Hello, body, what do you want and need?"

When you feel ready, open your eyes. Take a moment to come back into your body before proceeding with your day.

Bonus exercise: Amp up the practice by giving your body a nod of gratitude for carrying you through this crazy beautiful world. Maybe acknowledge your body for going about most of its functions without you even having to try.

As you become more accustomed to doing body scans, you will be able to quickly assess your body's needs throughout the day or stop to do these fuller attentive scans when they are needed.

Still feeling stuck after your scan? Consider adding flow by drinking more water, moving, and stretching. Slow, intentional movements in the body feel good and are helpful for its optimal functioning.

Do yoga. Dance. What needs to be shaken out? Let it go. Is it time to put on music? Sing?

Can you feel a difference? If you can't at first, that's OK. You are making inroads by paying attention at a deeper level. Creating good lines of communication can take a bit of time. You will get there, and you will experience positive results!

This is an exercise we will be building on, so implement it into your daily life flow now. Feeling resistance? If you prefer ignoring your body, it might be time to look more deeply at why that would be. You are worthy. Your body deserves all the love, attention, and respect it can be given. What voices are telling you otherwise?

Admiring Natural Beauty

Time to stop and enjoy some beauty. Healing and nourishment can happen any time we bring our attention in the direction of seeing our connection with the world around us. Did you know that the simple act of enjoying nature's beauty offers physiological benefits to the body, regardless of whether you do it in nature or online? Isn't the mind amazing?

Give yourself the time in nature that you feel you need. You will benefit from a few minutes, and you will reap even greater benefits from twenty. If you are enjoying a real life beauty moment, resist the temptation to snap a picture or share your moment to social media. Please let this break be undocumented. This is just for you, and keeping it for yourself will allow you to get more from the experience.

If you cannot get out into nature, there are endless videos on the internet that will give you access to every imaginable natural element you could desire visiting.

Perhaps you want to take a virtual tour of the Rockies in fall. Maybe a waterfall in paradise is more your speed. Or a stroll through the redwoods may appeal. It is all there, so just type in some keywords and go.

You will feel soothed, more relaxed, and less anxious. Ahhh…

Notice what images you are drawn to. Are you attracted to certain colors or elements in nature?

Beauty breaks! I relish beauty break time, because I know that despite any stress or anxiety I am feeling, even just looking out the window at the swaying trees or passing clouds will incite a sense of inner calmness that nourishes me.

I want those moments for you, too, if you're not currently taking time for them.

If you do not frequently make time to enjoy nature, your soul is aching for beauty breaks, whether or not it is in your consciousness. Spending time in nature has many expected, and maybe unexpected benefits.

A simple walk around natural elements will calm your nervous system, reduce stress, and ease your mind.

Did you know that while you are in nature your body lowers blood pressure, boosts your immune system, and even reduces inflammation in your body? Every single one of those physical benefits also increases your sexual wellness potential.

Your basic wellness depends upon your ability to relax and enjoy yourself. And while it may seem like a stretch, your ability to connect with and appreciate something as simple as the beauty of natural elements can and will translate to an overall increased sense of enjoyment in your body.

I find nature juicy. The ocean and jungle are particularly luscious places for me. Dewy, earthy with florals and saltiness. Mmmmm…

What would feel most nourishing to you? Your body knows what it needs to heal your body, mind and emotions. Tune inward and trust your intuition.

Start incorporating more beauty breaks into your day and notice how they leave you feeling.

Grounding and Earthing

Did you love to walk barefoot as a child? Or were you raised in an urban environment that kept shoes and cement between you and direct contact with the Earth? I really believe that our bodies long for natural connections, and this is one of the most basic ways to indulge in that need.

Begin with a basic grounding exercise.

Are you already familiar with grounding exercises? If not, let's delve into why grounding techniques can be incredibly helpful for de-stressing the body, soothing the nervous system, and keeping you more balanced and in the moment.

Energy needs to be grounded. Electricity does not work unless it is grounded, and humans operate better when their personal energy is grounded. Learning to be grounded will be particularly helpful for later exercises. It's a nice trick to have up your sleeve when you start feeling overwhelmed. I use grounding exercises in the morning, and anytime I start to feel off-balance. Grounding helps me feel more in the moment, operating at my best.

When you are grounded, you are not as likely to be thrown off-balance by surprises or stressors that come your way. Being grounded provides an anchor into the present moment, and creates a better connection with the material world. A healthy relationship with the material world will allow you to have a better understanding of your place in the world. This connection brings a wealth of benefits, from greater enjoyment of life to being a better manifestor. Test it out and see where improvements occur in your life.

This grounding technique takes very little time, and as long as you have a moment to safely close your eyes and ground your body, You will find that it can help you shake off frazzled feelings during stressful moments. Ground in and let that stressfully energy go!

While there are various ways to ground the body, there are some basic principles I have found to be important. Like the grounding rod we use to make sure electricity flows, you will be mentally anchoring yourself. I like to envision a cord from my tailbone through the layers of the ground, all the way down to the center of the Earth.

Another imagery I like to use is growing roots out of my feet. I see the roots growing deeper and deeper into the Earth. I send any stuck or unwanted energy that is in my body down through the cord or roots. This is a one-way flow. I send that energy out of my body into the Earth. This is an internal, intuitive process. You will know how much time to take with this practice, and the amount of time you need will likely vary depending on how much crud you need to release. Trust yourself.

My favorite visualization for grounding is to imagine becoming like a great rooted tree. Once you become more familiar and comfortable with a grounding practice you will be able to more quickly utilize it in various environments.

Basic Grounding Exercise:

If you have never used grounding techniques before, you will want to begin by bringing awareness into your physical body.

Sitting with your feet flat on the floor, close your eyes. Keep your spine straight. Bring awareness to your breath, which should be natural, not forced. As you inhale, relax your belly and allow air to flow into your body as a result of the expansion of the abdomen. You may want to put your hand on your belly to bring awareness there, as you continue to breathe. There are three parts to the breath: the inhale, the retention and the exhale. As you inhale, you are bringing life-giving energy into your body. With your exhale, imagine releasing any tension and negativity you may have accumulated in your body. Visualize sending this tension, negativity, and other energy that needs to be released, in a cord that goes from your tailbone to the center of the Earth. Take a few more breaths and with each exhale envision that cord getting brighter. When you are finished, give yourself a moment to come back into your body and the moment before moving on with your day.

Earthing Practice:

Want to connect even more deeply with Earth energy?

'Earthing', connecting with the Earth through the soles of the feet, has consistently been shown in studies to reduce stress, anxiety and feeling of depression; boost the immune system; improve sleep; and decrease inflammation. The premise is simple: direct contact with the mild negative charge of the Earth allows humans to reduce the excess of positive charge that can build up in the body, especially after long hours of being on electronics.

Take off your shoes, put your bare feet on dirt, lawn, sand, or whatever friendly terrain you have access to. Feel the Earth beneath your feet. Breathe. Close your eyes for an even deeper connection.

Continue taking slow, deep breaths, and as you relax into your body, notice any tension. As you exhale, imagine releasing the tension down through your feet and back into the Earth.

It has been my experience that about fifteen minutes is an optimal amount of time for a beneficial Earthing experience. But even five minutes can make a difference.

Do you feel more relaxed afterwards? Did it give you a sense of inner peace, or greater balance? Interestingly, this exercise can be an incredibly helpful sleep aid.

Letting Your Inner Child Pick a Pleasure

Life requires play, and having a playful attitude towards life can lighten and brighten the path.

Your soul is probably longing for this moment. Turn towards your inner source of joy. It is the cure for so many things that ail us.

We humans mistakenly tried to grow up and leave childhood activities behind. Turns out a lot of the childhood activities we enjoyed while growing up are the same things that keep our bodies and minds functioning well in adulthood, especially in later stages of life.

Inciting play, especially the activity most calling out from within you, can melt away stress, and soothe body, mind and spirit. You will feel refreshed, more relaxed and happier afterwards. Yay, you!

Pleasure is all about play.

Notice any resistance. Does the idea of playing like a child excite you, or does it sound stupid to you? Who told you to leave childhood activities in your childhood? After partaking in the play activity you choose, notice how it leaves you feeling.

What activity is right? The one that will get your inner child excited.

You almost can't go wrong with this one. Puzzles and artistic projects are not only relaxing for the nervous system and body, but they help stimulate the brain to keep it functioning well. Fort-making, kite-flying, and ball-playing are all great for you physically and physiologically. We have talked about and enjoyed the benefits of dancing, singing, and other playful experiences. Did doing any of this spark any playful desires in you?

Take at least an hour or two to play. Enjoy!

CHAPTER TWO

Legs - How We Carry Ourselves

In an ideal world we humans would be given ample room and encouragement to know and express our authentic selves in the outside world. Unfortunately, that is rarely the case.

Yet, it is integral to our growth to get to know ourselves. I mean *really* get to know ourselves. Have you begun to identify the narratives that consciously and unconsciously play out in your life, and which beliefs get you in trouble or can run amok? Are you aware of *why* you do what you choose to do each day? Do you understand your main motivations?

Unfortunately, the less we know and understand our own thoughts, beliefs and behaviors, the more easily we can be swayed by the outside world. Fortunately, self-knowledge can be a tether to keep one from becoming lost or adrift. In a world full of opinions and beliefs about who we *should* be, knowing who you are is an integral anchor grounding you in your truths.

This chapter is an invitation to take a deeper look at the patterns in your life. By understanding yourself and the ways you are choosing to carry yourself in the world, you can begin returning to who you really are and want to be.

Let's begin. First, create a safe space where you can work through your thoughts and feelings. which I like to call the "compost pile".

Choosing a Compost Pile

Composting is the art of turning waste into fertilizer. In the first chapter you created a physical space for yourself, and now I am recommending that you create a space to work through the mental and emotional crud. You'll be creating an *emotional* compost pile.

Inner reflective time is necessary to know oneself. How have you chosen to carry yourself in the world? Knowing and understanding your motivations and your triggers will allow you to move past your internal limitations. Making peace with your past will free you to experience the fulfillment you desire, deserve and are so capable of experiencing. Gotta compost the crap to grow those flowers!

There are various wonderful ways to compost, but before we delve into form, let's set a few guidelines. First and foremost, there are to be no judgments at the compost pile. Just observe, allow feelings to come up, and then get them out. All feelings are valid here, but as brave explorers we do not wallow. We get it out so it can be transmuted. Get it out and walk away.

This playbook offers simple exercises, but they can work at deep levels. Even stepping into pleasure can bring up some unpleasant feelings that may have been pushed down. Finding freedom in your body might bring up thoughts and feelings that need to be heard, expressed, and released.

Choose a locale to work through what needs to be transmuted. We are turning the BS you have picked up along your human journey into fertilizer.

How do we compost? Does this mean you have to keep a journal? Well, as our world and own minds have expanded, so too are the ways we can "journal".

Traditional journaling, and the popular practice of stream-of-consciousness writing (just get it down, don't judge) are excellent ways to get to know yourself better, allowing for insights and breakthroughs. But they certainly are not the only ways. And since this playbook is all about play and exploration, I would love for you to find whatever feels most inviting to you.

I really enjoy being able to play it day-by-day when it comes to my compost pile. My preference has been for the "pile" to be in one physical place that supports multiple mediums. Maybe I want to write some words and draw a few symbols one day. And the next day I want to doodle or paint to gain better insight into meditative or dream reflections. The answer for me was a journal with thicker pages to support these multi-medium outlets.

What appeals most to you?

Maybe you like the writing process, and therefore a traditional journal appeals. I am a big fan and have used stream-of-conscious journaling for decades. Pick a journal that will support your lifestyle and allow you to take notes whenever the mood or muse calls.

Perhaps you are a poet, and succinctly grouping words as a way to express your feelings sounds like more fun to you. Wonderful. How can you best incorporate that into your life?

Don't have time for it, or prefer to make your voice heard, literally? Easy! Your smartphone likely has both a voice recording program and a voice-dictation note-taking program. Which is better for you?

Are you an artist? Or does a certain art form you have never tried appeal to you?

What sounds easy, doable, and fun? Secure the right paper and draw pictures each day. Pencils, pens, crayons? (Avoid chalk, and messy forms that won't hold up over time.) What will you draw? Maybe a single image wants your attention one day, and a field of flowers wants to be drawn the next. Don't judge, merely observe and transmute.

Paint. Unless you use paint pens, acrylics are probably the easiest way to use paint for a brief time each day with an excellent potential for composting results. Choose a heartier stock of paper that will allow for quick dry times so you aren't stuck waiting for your compost pile to dry.

Some days you may find yourself painting fairies or unicorns, other days you may create dark, shadowy images that help navigate the places needing some love. Believe me, I have those in my journal, too. We are human. Humans have all kinds of lightness and shadow, and that's normal.

Like many humans I used to fear my shadow self. Observing, getting to know and befriending these "disowned" parts of myself has brought a peacefulness and self-acceptance that has allowed me to enjoy life so much more.

As Carl Jung said, "To become conscious of [the shadow] involves recognizing dark aspects of the personality as present and real. This act is the essential condition for any kind of self-knowledge."

Guess what? You are darkness and light, and the sooner you can embrace all the aspects of yourself, the sooner you can transform your life. You are allowed to love all the parts of you. They make up who you are. By recognizing and embracing all the pieces that comprise yourself, you will free yourself.

The point of emotional composting is to be as creative as you want to be, as long as it provides a judgment-free place to work through the stuff that needs to leave your mind/body/consciousness so that crud can be transmuted into something that supports your health and wellbeing. If at any point the thoughts or emotions that arise feel too overwhelming for you, please seek professional help. Asking for help when it is needed is brave and always the right thing to do.

Returning to Who You Really Are

As humans we love to tell stories and share myths. For many ancestral human years on Earth, stories and myths allowed us to understand where we came from and gave us a sense of purpose and belonging. The stories allowed us to see where we fit in and gave us a sense of identity. Sometimes humans found that expectations from those around them were the right fit, and other times they were not. That's the down-side to expectations.

Humans are prone to latching onto other's stories and myths. For good or bad, we humans can let the voices of others become narratives in our own minds. Sometimes we latch onto meaning we haven't been able to find or allow for ourselves. This can lead to over-identification with a certain story or stories. We humans, as a collective, have struggled long and hard with our attachment to narratives. Many of us don't even realize how much we let them dictate our lives.

For as strong and hearty as humans can be, we can just as equally be easily hurt. A voice on the playground, a flippant remark in the locker room, or even a comment from a loved one in our home can become a lifetime mental bully replaying in our own minds.

The remedy for over-identification is a willingness to name the story being played out, and consciously working to change the thinking patterns that keep those narratives from playing out in the over-identifier's life.

I have found it helpful to playfully 'nod' to these voices when they creep into my mind. You might try your own version of acknowledging undesired messages as they try to play out in your mind (more on this in chapter six). Saying, "Oh, I see you" to negative thinking patterns as they arise is a way to take your own power back.

How have you allowed certain stories or voices to play out in your life? Where did those stories come from? What purpose do they serve? Are they bringing you a sense of fulfillment? Or are they keeping you from experiencing what is meaningful for you?

Our societies can be weird to navigate, and sometimes it can be easier to put on a facade. Our world often requires various versions of ourselves. These pretenses allow us to blend in, which tends to protect us from negative attention. These false identities, or masks, can be a common human coping mechanism to combat fears about not fitting in, not being able to fulfill the expectations placed upon us, or just to survive. Many of us learn early in our human experience that "being oneself" can have negative consequences.

Sometimes being oneself could have deadly costs in this world. It is a horrible truth; the result of expectations, rules, and beliefs that are exclusionary of lifestyles that do not fit within the cultural norms deemed "acceptable".

Only you know if you are being true to you. How often are you really being yourself? Maybe you aren't even sure of the answer to that. I would never ask you to take actions that would endanger you in any way. What I am asking you to do with this exercise is to get honest with *yourself*.

We must continuously take stock of the stories we allow to play out in our lives as humans, or they will just keep playing out over and over again. How unfortunate.

How are you carrying yourself in the world, and does it work for you?

Focus the microscope to look at your life's main patterns and themes. What same narratives continually play out in your life? Pay special attention to the stories you have about pleasure and your own body as a sexual being. Upcoming exercises are designed to assist you with clearing up messages you may have been given around these normal, natural human experiences. Other people's beliefs, stories, and expectations will only hinder your ability to experience pleasure in your body. Pleasure is your birthright, and only you get to write the story of how that will play out for you. You have to know yourself and what is in your heart to be able to intentionally create the life you desire and deserve. Releasing untruths will allow you to fully partake in real life enjoyment.

Assessment Questions to Consider:

- If your life had three main themes, what words would you use to describe those themes?
- Were you expected to follow another's expectations for your life? Or have you followed your own dreams?
- How many of the pivotal moments in your life came from genuine self-calling?
- Do you feel as though you are on your true life path?
- Has your sexuality been allowed free expression? If not, how has that left you feeling?
- What is the biggest change you would like to make in your life? What's keeping you from making that change?

There are ever better dreams to have for one's life, my Love. Just make sure you are working towards things for *you*. It's a short life, after all, and I want the best for you. I certainly hope you do, too. Dream big. You deserve it all!

Please work through the mental and emotional feelings that arise in your compost pile. Free yourself! Let it go.

Shedding Body Shame

Let's talk about body shame.

Humans are not born with shame. Shame is learned here on Earth.

We are taught to feel ashamed of body parts, and behavior around our own bodies. Sexual bodily shame is common around the world.

By a young age most humans have come to feel uncomfortable or unhappy with some of their body parts. This discomfort can easily (and is often) carried into adulthood.

We can wear body shame like an uncomfortable extra set of skin - a shame suit - cloaking us. Inside is often a small insecure child, begging for reassurance, validation, and love. That uncomfortably fitting suit lives in the energetic-body. But make no mistake, just because you can't visibly see it, doesn't mean it isn't making itself visible in your life.

Body shame and insecurities can have a huge impact in how we carry ourselves in the world.

If there is a child who believes they are not safe and secure in their own body, the desire to fill that void often leads to seeking outwardly for that validation. It is incredibly common for humans to search for validation from the world around them. This can lead to unhealthy habits that may temporarily fill the void but can become even more problematic. Unhealthy habits may change form, but they do tend to grow until they've been brought to consciousness where they can be acknowledged and healed.

Unhealthy habits often leave people with feelings of guilt, frustration, and additional shame. How, then, could one ever be expected to experience real, deep, and fulfilling pleasure in one's body? How would one be able to create authentic and meaningful relationships?

How have so many of us acquired this body shame? Easily. We pick up comments made socially and culturally from within our families, neighborhoods, communities, media, and social media. Shame can be picked up and passed down from generation to generation because shame is woven into belief systems.

That means that shame can become a part of your energetic-body very early on.

When we arrive upon the scene of this human experience, we have zero shame, and it is wonderful.

We play, explore, and learn. Watch any baby and you will notice that we humans discover our genitals and pleasure very quickly. Many babies touch their genitals while in the womb, because it feels good, and can be comforting. It is in our human nature to follow what feels pleasurable. We are born with a neurologically wired-in trusty guide whose intention it is to lead us towards that which is nourishing and healthy for us.

Even parents with a positive outlook on sexuality can pass down shame that they themselves were taught. Most humans have their hands guided away from touching their genitals when they do so as babies. Most humans are raised with shame around deriving pleasure from their genitals. When humans are taught to feel embarrassed and wrong for touching their genitals, these negative messages can become problematic in adulthood.

In many cultures masturbation has long been labeled as 'sinful' and 'shameful'. Some beliefs dictate that it is impure to even *think* about pleasurable activities, especially if those activities involve other humans. So, despite mountains of scientific data and human experiences showing that enjoying pleasure in our bodies is healthy for us, we are taught instead to feel guilt. This sense of doing something wrong gets passed down generationally, and the shame continues to hinder the potential for enjoying our inherent sexual nature.

Maybe your parents raised you with beliefs that slapped labels like 'dirty' or 'sin' on the human form. How could anyone feel good about that? I mean, seriously. We have put some hardcore rules on the *right* way to be a human. The common ideals and standards we are taught that we *should* live by don't even match up with our core neurological wiring, which is there to help our bodies stay healthy.

Another way we humans can take on body shame and discomfort is through comparisons and societal beauty ideals.

Observe cultures around the globe and you will find that while the ideals may differ, most humans live with certain value systems around how humans *should* look. Each culture holds certain ideals of what has been deemed physically superior beauty.

One might hope that we would enjoy living in a world where humans are not all the same, and even celebrate those differences. We would cherish the gift of being in bodies that can change throughout our lives and appreciate the gifts each stage of being human brings. We would teach little humans that the only "ideal" body is a healthy one, and that enjoying pleasure is a natural and important part of a wellness plan. Ahh my daydream for us all, but until then…

As humans connected through the world wide web, beauty ideals have become modern day idolizing. Hello, pop culture in a social media-driven world. Well, guess what? That's not serving us, and it is time for a wake-up call before more get harmed by unrealistic expectations.

Why do we even want to be the same, or look like some cultural ideal? It's ridiculous. Who's even picking these images for us? Why are we buying into it?

I personally wasted years on adjusting my look in subtle ways to try to "fit in". I want a refund on those years. It's tragic. In my teen years I tried to lighten my naturally red strawberry-blonde hair so I could have a more beach-chic California look. In my early 20's I tried to fake tan and hide away my fair English skin. I also hid my curves and tried to amplify areas that didn't exist. This lack of self-acceptance and love definitely didn't contribute to my ability to live a happy life. Fortunately, I learned to accept all of myself, just as I am.

What other influences contribute to our insecurities? They can come from a show on TV, a silly video, or an article. Social media is constantly contributing to false ideals that stir up insecurities. Sadly, many times a lack of self-acceptance comes from a conversation or comment from a friend or family member. That garbage can really stick in your head and becomes a new part of the shame suit you wear around.

I can still remember a conversation that took place decades ago between the matriarchs in my family. It was a rare reunion for a cousin's wedding, and four generations of women were in attendance. I was a blossoming sixteen-year-old young woman, and I still remember the outfit I was wearing. Isn't it funny what stays in your mind? I wore a two-piece; long skirt and long-sleeved top. The material was quality cotton with some lycra, so the outfit clung to my newly developing curves. And while it covered me and showed very little skin, its emphasis on my hips had caught the older matriarchs' attention.

"She has hips," one of them noted.

I was asked to turn around. "She has the family satchel ass," another female family member chimed in. There were nods and agreements. The message was clear: Poor Antonia, she has wide hips.

"She'll be able to birth babies, though," someone said.

"Good thing, she'd be a bean pole otherwise," an older matriarch remarked.

Those matriarchs have all left this realm now, and I long ago forgave them. However I did carry a lot of shame about my bootie for years. One year in my twenties, I returned from a beautiful beach vacation and stupidly took a black marker to any pictures that showed my womanly hips and backside.

Ironically, we now live in a world where booties and hips are celebrated. I don't believe that one single lover I have had in this lifetime felt that my hips were anything but beautiful and sexy. It took some work, but I did grow to appreciate and love my hips and my booty. That liberation, in my day-to-day life and the bedroom, have made an invaluable contribution to my happiness and pleasure.

But there were other body parts with which I needed to make peace. As I grew into my adult body, I was told that it had additional inadequacies.

Magazines, television, advertising, and even partners with whom I intimately shared my body somehow all had an opinion about what an ideal body should look like, and mine didn't always measure up. Perhaps you can relate?

None of us can ever measure up if we seek validation from outside of ourselves, or buy into these unrealistic narratives.

Feelings about body inadequacies can go a lot of places, and rarely is it going to be healthy or empowering.

Today is the day we change that.

Letting go of body shame is going to be invaluable to you, because that sad heavy weight has been carried around for long enough. Ready to feel lighter?

You are beginning a love affair with your body, and that is going to transform your life in a myriad of amazing ways, including allowing yourself to finally feel at home in your body, as it should be. You will start enjoying your body more. Hooray! Acceptance leads to true self-confidence, which will also help you create better connections with others, especially intimate partners.

You have to be willing to stand up to any inner bullies and shut them down. Today is the day that love is bigger than fear. You are ready. It is time to love your body just as it is, right here and now. It is important that you believe in yourself. You can do this, my brave pleasure-seeking Friend!

Releasing Body-Shame Exercise:

Do this exercise by yourself, wherever you would like, as long as it feels like a safe space where you will not be interrupted.

Sitting at a desk or table would be great for this. It could also be done on the couch or in bed.

You can use your compost pile for this, or a large piece of paper, preferably with a marker. Set these supplies on the nearby desk, table, etc.

Sit down, close your eyes. You will be using your non-judgmental mind for this experience. Merely observe, acting as a witness to this human life experience of yours.

Go back in time to the earliest human experience you can remember in this lifetime.

Just notice what you see, like you are watching this on television. Merely observe.

What shame has this sweet, innocent, beautiful little human picked up along their human journey?

Allow your mind to skip from moment to moment in your life, just noticing what wants to be seen. What was the messaging you got along the way? Just notice as words come up. Keep moving forward on the timeline until you are back in the present.

Open your eyes and start writing those words down on the piece of paper. Don't overthink.

What shame do you carry? What messages are engrained on that skin that has been energetically weighing you down? Get that crud out like you are mega composting!

When you are finished, take a moment to just be with the words and phrases that came up.

Stand up, take your paper with you, and face your full-length mirror. Drop your robe and hold the paper towards yourself (not the mirror), so you can read it. Look back at your beautiful self.

This is the body carrying you through in this lifetime. Your body is a gift. Self-acceptance of this naturally beautiful body will change your life, my Love.

Think back to when you were that sweet, innocent small human. Use the lens of a compassionate, loving best friend.

Look back at the mirror, put your hand on your heart and speak all of the loving words you deserve and need to hear. Maybe you want to tell yourself how sorry you are for the negative messages that got placed on you. Feelings are likely to arise. Great. Are you angry, sad, or do you find yourself laughing? There is no right or wrong, as long as you come back to a place in yourself that can offer the respect, love and deep honoring your body deserves for being the vessel that allows you to have this human experience at all.

This is the one body you have been given in this lifetime. It will change, and it won't always be easy to watch those changes as they occur. Love yourself. Every bit of you, just as you are right now.

We all are all beautiful humans. We are all deserving because we were born. Making peace with your body and releasing shame you were taught is liberating. Yessss! Finally!

Lowering Energy: Finding Comfort with Stillness

Today you get to lie down and just relax. How simple is that?

What does the ability to relax have to do with how you carry yourself in the world? Most of us have forgotten how to truly relax in the body. We have become so occupied by our busyness that we have forgotten the importance of its wellness-rich cousin, nothingness.

Scientific studies have consistently shown the health benefits of stillness, so much so that world-renowned medical communities have recommended that humans put relaxation at the top of their priority lists. But do we listen? No, we are too busy!

Balance is integral for being a truly happy human, especially in a world that is constantly vying for our attention in ways that can easily distract or throw us off balance. We weren't built for the overwhelming amount of information we are absorbing. As a result our brains filter out what we deem "less important". So next time you start forgetting details you would normally be on top of, notice if it is the likely result of mental and/or emotional overwhelm. It's OK. It just means that you are in need of some relaxation and integration time.

As everything is energy, including us, it can be helpful to notice when you are raising or lowering energy. There is validity in both, but keeping yourself balanced means tuning in to notice which your body is craving - uplifting and raising your energy, or lowering energy and turning inward through stillness.

Perhaps you are a part of a religious or spiritual community that advocates for relaxation. Many religious belief systems incorporate a day of rest in their philosophies. But still many of us do not give our body/mind/spirit's need for rest the proper respect, appreciation, and time it deserves.

When you hear "just relax" does it feel like a trigger for you?

The directive to "relax" is all too often used when a human expresses an emotion intensely, or acts in a way that is triggering to other humans. Outbursts are often met with, "Just relax". The message behind the directive is usually that something is wrong with our behavior. It is understandable then that 'relax' can become a trigger word instead of being seen as a welcome opportunity.

But relaxing is a HUGE wellness tool for humans, so it is time to let old associations with the word go. Relaxing, and the ability to relax, is gold. GOLD. It is simple, but incredibly important.

You may find a greater sense of peace and relaxation in your body. Thoughts are likely to arise. Feelings will pop up, too. It's all perfect.

Let's talk about what constitutes relaxing, shall we? For your purposes today, the desired result is for you to let go of your thoughts and just be. I hope that sounds as soothing as it actually can be for you. You get to just relax, and do nothing. Ahhh, yeah!

Unfortunately, just being still can make humans incredibly uncomfortable. Fear not, this merely indicates a greater need to work with and explore ways to rest up.

All you need is a place where you can safely and comfortably lie down, breathe, and not be disturbed for ten blissful minutes.

Find a comfortable position, preferably on your back. Tune in and position your body as needed to allow for real relaxation.

Breathe. Notice if breathing makes space for greater states of relaxation. Just be.

Watch thoughts. Don't try to push thoughts away. But for real relaxation to happen, it would be beneficial to sit with the thoughts that make you feel good. Negative feelings may arise, and that is OK. Simply return your focus back to imagining good stuff in that head of yours. Happy thoughts. Notice the difference in your body as you shift your focus towards joy.

When negative thoughts creep in, and they will, just notice then switch your focus. Is that challenging? It is normal for humans to struggle with letting go of their thinking state, and even more so when the focus is on positive things. So, lean toward just feeling good. That's it. Breathe. Just relax.

Raising and Resonating Energy - Making Your Playbook Soundtracks

It is time to bring in music. You will be making two playlists, with a minimum of 6 songs, 12 songs max per playlist, for simplicity's sake. You will be making an uplifting playlist, and another of music that you find to be soothing and relaxing. You might also find it helpful to create a third playlist of sensual songs for sexy time.

Time to tap into your inner DJ skills and harness the power of music for your personal pleasure. Don't worry if you cannot think of what music elevates or relaxes you - there are pre-made lists to turn to.

Music is an instant mood setting device. Music is an easy way to create a joyful, relaxing or sensual feel. Listening to the right tunes can also be an excellent anchor to get you out of your head.

You will be utilizing music for the incredible health and wellness tool it can be. Let the feelings in your body guide the way. Only you know what's going to be the right fit for you. Don't get stuck on any one song or list. Change up the lists as often as you like. This is all for your pleasure, after all.

The world around us uses music to affect our moods. Why shouldn't we?

From movies and television shows, to the music at the grocery store and in elevators. Music is often present around us, consciously chosen for how it will make us feel.

After all, everything is energy that is resonating in some way in our bodies. Have you ever had the experience of wanting to listen to a certain song over and over again, only to listen to it later and have it irritate you and set you on edge?

We all understand the power of music. Studies support the wide array of benefits listening to music can provide, including physical, psychological, neurological, and even social benefits.

Trust me, you will want some solid beats to carry you through many of the exercises you will be doing in the following chapters. Maybe you already have playlists made, but I would prefer you create new ones. Songs can stir up emotions, so choose new songs specifically with the intention to relax or uplift you.

For your first list choose your tried and true uplifting songs that will get you moving and dancing. Uplifting music has been shown to increase blood flow, which has many added measurable benefits, including being good for your heart. Healthy blood flow is imperative for good health, including genital wellness and functioning. Ready to move that body now?

Listening to music has also been shown to boost dopamine production. Studies have shown that music can trigger the brain to release chemicals that distract the body from pain, just like orgasms do. All of this is helpful for fun playground activities!

What else should you consider while making these playlists? For the uplifting playlist, choose at least one song that you can't help but sing along to. Choose another that gets your hips moving. For me that is often something Latin flavored, especially Cuban. For you it might be something very different. All is welcome, as long as it lifts your mood, makes you feel lighter, happier and makes you want to move that body of yours.

For the second playlist, you'll be choosing chill songs. Think spa or elevator music, but in whatever form resonates for you. Maybe you prefer classical music. I want this to be a pleasurable experience for you.

What makes you say, "ahhh…" and relax into your body when you hear it? Add that! Go from there.

When you have time, make a third playlist. Create a sensual playlist for sexy activities. What music gets you in the mood, and will lend a sultry vibe to your pleasure playground?

No clue where to begin? Many other humans around the world probably have you covered. Start searching playlists on the platform where you prefer to listen to music. You can use keywords such as 'chill', 'relax' and 'upbeat'. Happy playlist making!

Dancing Your Way Through the World

Movement is a great way to check in with your body, release tension, play and have fun.

Dancing is an incredible mood elevator. It's also an incredible way to get in touch with and move through emotions.

We humans move our bodies for pleasure before we are even born. Most babies and young humans love to move and flow with music or fun sounds. Did you find dance pleasurable as a child? Dancing is an ancient remedy. If you think about it, all of life is a dance, and flowing with the rhythm within you is a wonderful way to make your life more fun.

Dancing is another way to build new neural pathway networks based on pleasure instead of stress. Oh, yeah!

My love for dance began early in life. I have been moving my body for the pleasure of it for most of my life.

I never excelled in structured dance classes. But during my more challenging college years I found expressive movement. It is movement without thought, or a need for form. I found the intuitive dance style to be an incredible wellness tool for me. I was able to dance and sweat out my stress, or joyfully celebrate.

Whichever dance form calls to you, there are many benefits awaiting you.

There are physiological, physical, and emotional benefits to dance. Dance makes us feel good because it gets the body to kick out feel-good hormones like endorphins. Dancing helps keep the body strong, flexible and balanced, all of which are advantageous, especially in the bedroom.

As we go about our busy lives, stuff we may not have time to deal with can get shoved down in our bodies. Trapped energy, awaiting release. Dance is a great way to loosen and remove this energy. Dancing can also be a great confidence booster, which can beneficially change one's relationship with oneself and the outside world.

Turn on an uplifting song from your playlist and explore dance movement for yourself. If you are already prone to having solo dance parties, try deepening your practice by exploring a new form of dance and movement.

CHAPTER THREE

Hips and Pelvis - Home of Creativity, Angst and Orgasmic Possibilities

When was the last time you thought about your relationship with your pelvis area? It's not a welcomed topic in most societies. But, have you ever considered how much power exists in those hips of yours?

The sacral area is the seat of creativity. The fabric of existence is sexual creative energy. Unfortunately many belief systems around the globe have hindered our ability to tap into this essential part of life experience. Instead of embracing this natural part of ourselves, we are taught shame and discomfort that can lead to a great deal of angst.

By making peace with our inherent sexuality, we open ourselves to a well of creative energy and endless pleasure. One should never underestimate how one's relationship with sexuality is playing out in every area of one's life. This is a biggie, my Friend.

Humans are born uninhibited, but by a young age many learn to have guilt around sexuality.

This chapter offers ways to free yourself of hang-ups that could be preventing you from enjoying all of the pleasure you are capable of experiencing.

You may find yourself triggered. If you do, or if insights arise, make note of them and work through thoughts and emotions at the compost pile. You have a wealth of tools here to assist you - trust yourself to turn to the perfect practice(s) you need. Be gentle with yourself. Keep an open mind and compassionate heart.

Redefining 'Sex' and 'Orgasm'

Before we delve into an honest inquiry of sexuality, let's define a couple of basic human experiences. Taking a moment to touch in with ubiquitous and often charged terms such as 'sex' can offer opportunities for healing. When was the last time you reflected on your personal associations with the words 'sex' and 'orgasm'? Consider whether these definitions may need some personal (and societal) redefining.

Associations with terminology can be quite impactful on one's thinking and life, especially one's intimate life.

What is an 'Orgasm'?

Merriam-Webster defines 'orgasm' as "intense or paroxysmal excitement".

Well that doesn't sound very fun to me.

The definition continues, perhaps a bit more invitingly, "especially: the rapid pleasurable release of neuromuscular tensions at the height of sexual arousal that is usually accompanied by the ejaculation of semen in the male and vaginal contractions in the female".

What is important about the first part of the definition is that an orgasm does not, in fact, *need* to be genitally focused. We humans have definitely limited our potential by thinking that orgasmic pleasure *has* to be derived from a penis or vulva/vagina. In fact, this narrow thinking has done us all quite a disservice.

Humans have sexualized orgasms. However, evidence shows that humans are experiencing orgasms in non-sexual ways. This disparity can make things a bit confusing when we experience intense moments of orgasmic-like pleasure derived in other ways.

As it turns out, there are a myriad of ways to have orgasms.

Perhaps you have read one of the many articles about the "10 Types of Orgasms" a human with a vulva/vagina can experience. While that may help broaden our perceptions of what is orgasmically possible, it can also be equally limiting. Why should a human be able to have a nipplegasm (from stimulation of a nipple) or a coregasm (from the core of the body, often while exercising) but not have an orgasm from stimulation of a toe or earlobe? All of it is possible.

Since science has proven that humans can "think" their way to orgasm, wouldn't it be possible that oral stimulation such as eating a delicious piece of chocolate could incite orgasm? It is not really that far-fetched. Plenty of humans have detailed such experiences. I experienced an orgasm from eating mango once. It wasn't sexual, but it felt lovely. Why do we have to make these natural experiences weird?

If we began to desexualize orgasm and made peace with the many ways orgasms can be derived, we would infinitely expand possibilities for experiencing pleasure. It might also allow us to feel more comfortable sharing our experiences with others.

A small percentage of humans are unable to orgasm despite adequate stimulation and efforts, which is known as anorgasmia. Anorgasmia is reported more commonly by humans with vagina/vulvas than it is by penis-havers. Maybe orgasmic-like satisfaction can be found from an unexpected body part, or in a unique way?

What is 'Sex'?

Let's talk about how humans have defined 'sex', because our limited definition is both confusing and creating societal issues.

Modern society frequently still defines 'sex' as the penetrative act of a penis entering a vagina. This leaves out many human's preferred sexual experiences. In addition to discounting human genders and orientations, defining sex through such a simplistic heteronormative lens leaves out many sexual acts. Oral sex, anal sex, fingering, and other forms of genital and anal play should be included in the definition of 'sex'.

When we can be more inclusive of experiences humans are having and widen our perceptions of what is possible in the body, we can more easily make peace with these natural human experiences.

Reflective Questions You May Want to Consider:

- What associations do you have for the terms 'orgasm' and 'sex'?
- Where could there be healing to allow you to make peace with these terms?
- Would having wider definitions for these terms have been helpful to you in your teen and young adult years?
- What negative emotions arise in you when you consider your personal experiences with orgasms and sex?
- Where could healing happen to allow you to make peace with your personal sexual and orgasmic experiences?

Embracing Yourself as a Sexual Being

We are told many stories about the human body as we grow up. Some of those stories we take on as our own. Some influence us even when we know they are not true. But we can always re-evaluate our beliefs and rewire our brains with new thinking.

One of the biggest patterns that can trip us up where sexuality is concerned is around the messages we received about our bodies and sexual pleasure.

Humans raise their little humans to know "right" from "wrong", and what is "good" and "bad". We humans have rules about life and trying to teach little humans that something that comes completely natural to them, such as touching genitals just because it feels good, can be a very complicated thing.

Were you given healthy messages about touching your body, or were you shamed for it?

It is time to look at what you believe about yourself as a sexual being. What you really believe. And why.

It is also time to let go of the myths and untruths about yourself as a sexual being, so you can finally relax and enjoy the body you are in.

As you answer the questions below, notice what other narratives arise. Breathe. Use your resources and compost pile as needed.

When you have finished, please re-read the Playground Truths at the beginning of this book.

Use These Questions to Begin Your Inquiry:

- What did you learn about sexuality throughout your childhood? Were you taught that sex is a normal, natural part of being human?
- Were you given negative messages around sexuality? If so, how have these beliefs impacted your life and intimate relationships?
- What were your experiences of your first time having intercourse?
- Describe each of your parents' sex lives in a few words. Is there a theme?

- What other sexual experiences have shaped your current beliefs about sexuality?
- What would your most delicious, ideal sex-life look and feel like?

Understanding Your Sex Drive

Making peace with your sex drive, as it is, can give you the space to start enjoying more pleasures in all areas of your life.

Many humans think of a sex drive as a set measurable drive, one either does or does not have. The human sex drive naturally fluctuates throughout our lifetimes. Having higher or lowered sex drives at varying times is perfectly normal. It's a pity we stress out and beat ourselves up about this natural fluctuation.

Sexuality is complex, with many variables including: physically, physiologically, psychologically, relationally. Each of these can add to, and decrease, desire or "drive". Certain medical conditions can change a sex drive, as can the use of medications. When a human experiences a sudden loss of desire (that had previously been present), ruling out medical reasons is often the first step in assessing the reason for the loss in sex drive.

As hormones play an important role in drive, humans often find that drive can be higher during puberty and again in their late 20's or 30's. This varies considerably from human to human. Hormonal changes during pregnancy and after giving birth can also contribute to fluctuations in desire.

Physiologically, stress can have a strong impact on changes in drive. Studies indicate that smaller amounts of stress can amplify sex drive, while greater amounts of stress and anxiety often decrease desire. Stress is very frequently the culprit when a human who had a sex drive experiences a sudden decrease in desire.

Neuroscientists have shown that human sex drive has a real *use it or lose it* component. Studies show that when you have more sex, you want more sex. Want to experience greater desire? You have to make more time for pleasure.

Congratulations! You have already been doing just that. Have you noticed your desire growing? It happens organically when your body feels nourished by healthy pleasures in the body, and as the result of decreased stress levels. If it isn't happening for you yet, that's OK.

What To Do When Sex Drives Don't Match Up:

Are you partnered? If you are, you may be stressed that your sex drives are not matching up. Unfortunately, because sex drives naturally fluctuate, desire doesn't always match up between committed partners.

If you are the one with the higher drive, it is important not to put pressure on your partner if they are not feeling the same way. It is equally important not to make yourself feel bad about wanting sex more than your partner does. Unfortunately, being the one with the higher drive can lead to feelings of rejection, which can get frustrating. Your partner is probably having similar feelings. Remember that mismatched drives can be a difficult and a tender situation for you both. Adding pressure for sex is likely to add to their frustrations, which could put stress on your relationship.

Our culture doesn't always provide this message, but our sexuality is always our own personal responsibility. What are you needing, and how can you respectfully take care of these needs?

Being honest with yourself about your needs and desires is the first step as it will allow you to have the honest conversation with your partner that you both deserve. Being willing to have an open discussion about the situation will help take the pressure off what can otherwise become a mounting issue.

How does one even initiate such a conversation?

Have a conversation in a safe, uninterrupted space like a living room, rather than in the bedroom. Approach the conversation from a place of friendship. These conversations are often a relief, because you are both aware of the situation, and not talking about it creates tension. Hopefully having a much needed conversation brings you closer together.

Try to use first-person, non-blaming "I feel" statements. Do not begin sentences with triggering words like "you make me" or "you always", which is only likely to make your partner defensive. Don't dwell on the issue. Stay solution-focused: "How can we make this better?"

Talk things through calmly and compassionately. Being honest about your sexual needs and desires can be a great way to build intimacy or get clear about what is not working. Just because your sex drives are not aligned doesn't mean that your relationship is doomed. It may be scary to talk about, but you will both feel better when you do.

Yes, you aren't matching up sexually. Where *can* you comfortably meet each other?

If you are the one with the lower drive, what *is* within your comfort zone? Starting with small shared pleasures without pressure for sex can be a great place to comfortably begin for many couples. If you are the one with the lower drive, it is equally important for you not to beat yourself up about it. What are you needing from your partner in the way of intimacy? The trick is to make your solution a pressure-free, fun experience for you both.

You may find it helpful to schedule a date with sex off the table. Keeping the focus on simply reconnecting with each other can be a great start. What do you two enjoy doing together? Or, what have you two always wanted to do together? How can you creatively implement those activities into your lives?

Scheduling sex doesn't sound sexy, but it can be a great solution for a lot of couples when energy levels aren't synced. Put date nights on your calendar and then bring your a-game by dressing up for the occasion and flirting like you did when you first met. Bringing in the elements of playfulness and flirtation goes a long way. Also, never underestimate the power of genuine appreciation! Everyone wants to feel loved and appreciated, and these heartfelt connections can be truly transformative.

Still not connecting? There are lots of counselors available online now, so don't hesitate to reach out and get assistance if you and/or your partner feel you need it.

In the meantime, masturbation can be an excellent way to take away any pressure on the person with the lower drive, while reducing frustrations for the person with the higher drive. Being honest about sexual needs opens the door for solutions and masturbating when a partner isn't in the mood is often the best option. Because, again, our sexuality is always in our own hands.

Perhaps the person with the lower drive wants to watch or join you while you masturbate. If so, would having a prior agreement to remove any sexual expectations be helpful? If they are comfortable with it, mutual masturbation can be a fantastic (and sexy) way to build intimacy.

What if You Have Never Experienced a Sex Drive, or Want a Break From Sex?

A small percentage of humans on this planet are born with no sex drive and have no interest in sexual activities, which is known as 'asexuality'.

Asexuality is not a lifestyle choice. It should not be confused with abstinence. Research has shown that there is no evidence that asexuality is a psychological or mental disorder. Asexuality is also not caused by a chemical imbalance. Rather asexuality is seen as an inherent predisposition because asexuals show an innate, early onset, and lifelong lack of sexual attraction that has not been caused by chemistry or traumatic sexual experiences. Asexuals were born just not feeling it, and many asexuals report frustration that the rest of the world is so focused on sex.

Our society places importance on sexual gratification, but many asexuals report experiencing intense pleasure and fulfillment through other sensory experiences. An asexual may have orgasmic-like satisfaction from non-sexual oral or tactile methods. These types of experiences are another reason that it is important to redefine 'orgasm'. By sexualizing the term, we exclude experiences humans are having and limit potentials.

Sexual abstinence is an intentional choice to wait by those who have not yet had sexual intercourse. Abstinence before marriage is a common religious choice in many cultures. Abstaining from sex is a valid choice, as long as it is chosen for personal reasons rather than outside pressures. Ideally, abstaining allows one a safe space to ensure one is physically, psychologically and emotionally ready for sexual experiences.

Sometimes humans choose to refrain from having sex for a sustained period of time, which is known as "celibacy". Celibacy can be a common choice made after a human experiences a big life event such as a breakup, loss of a loved one, or having a child. Celibacy can also be common for spiritual and religious reasons. Taking breaks from sexual encounters can be a healthy choice. Following one's own internal guidance system about what feels right for one at a given point in one's life is often the best choice.

Taking Stock of Your Sex Drive Narrative:

- How has your desire for sex impacted your life and relationships?
- Do you feel good about your current sex drive? If not, what would you change?

- If partnered, have your sex drives matched up well, or have there been issues about desire levels?
- How has this playbook changed how you feel about your sex drive?
- What would you most like to gain from this playbook journey in regard to your sex drive?

Training Your Pelvic Floor

Do you know where your pubococcygeus muscle (PC) is located, and how to contract it?

The PC muscle allows you to maintain bladder control, have strong orgasms and increase sexual functioning. Strong PC muscles will also help you move sexual energy around your body. After the brain, the PC muscle is the most essential muscle for your sexual wellness and pleasure.

The pubococcygeus is the muscle in your pelvis that stretches from your pubic bone (in front) to your coccyx bone (in the back). This muscle resembles a little hammock, and is important because it forms the floor of your pelvic cavity and supports the pelvic organs. That means if it's strong and healthy it will make sure you go pee only when you want to, your sex organs will get proper blood flow, you will have better ejaculate control (especially helpful for those with a penis), and your orgasms can pack a far better punch.

With age, neglect or damage from surgery, excessive constipation or being overweight, the PC muscle can weaken. Birthing a baby puts understandable strain on the PC muscle. Many vagina-having humans experience issues, like situational urine leakage, due to unsupportive PC muscles. But the good news is that this wonderful little muscle can be exercised and kept in shape!

The concept of strengthening the pubococcygeus muscles first entered the Western world in the late 1940's when Dr. Arnold Kegel created Kegel exercises as a way for women to regain bladder control after childbirth had stretched or weakened the muscle area.

Today pelvic floor muscle training (PFMT) exercises are being recommended by doctors around the globe as a way to treat bladder control issues and improve sexual functioning for all humans.

There is limited research on the benefits of PFMT, particularly for penis-havers, but so far studies have been promising. PFMT has shown to be an effective method for successfully improving erections, ejaculation control, and for increasing orgasm intensity. As it happens, similar techniques have been used for centuries in Eastern parts of the world for the exact same purposes.

If you have not worked this muscle before, you can locate it by stopping the flow of urine the next time you are peeing. Do you notice the feel of the clenched muscles when you squeeze to stop the flow? That is your PC muscle.

It takes anywhere from a couple of weeks to months to tone the pubococcygeus muscles and begin noticing improvement as the muscles strengthen. More reps can shorten this time considerably.

It has been my experience that strengthening this sexual muscle is foundational to learning how to reach orgasm with muscle control alone, known as an energy-body orgasm or "thinking" oneself to orgasm.

Despite scientific evidence for the human ability to "think" oneself to orgasm, it is rarely discussed. So weird, right? I wish someone had told me my body was capable of such things long ago.

From personal experience, I can assure you without a doubt that the daily effort to strengthen the PC muscle is well worthwhile.

As you become more comfortable and adept with Kegel exercises, begin noticing if you sense your sexual energy being stirred as you squeeze and release. Is there an experience of arousal or pleasure? There may not be, and that's fine too. You never want to force sexual energy to move. It is merely an invitation, and you are just observing sensations in the body at this beginning stage. We will intentionally move sexual energy later in this playbook.

When you feel comfortable and adept at Kegel exercises, or if you already have a PFMT exercise routine, feel free to advance to the additional exercises detailed below. The PC pump and PC pull-up exercises can be utilized by any gender. I've included the "squeeze your way to more pleasure" exercise for clitoris-having participants.

The PFMT exercises you begin today will benefit you for the rest of your life!

PFMT Exercises

1. **Basic Kegel:** Begin by contracting your PC muscle, inhaling as it tightens. Inhale and hold, then relax as you exhale. Ideally you will be able to do this little series of tightening, holding, and releasing in a succession of twenty, with a ten second hold on each. Start by doing just ten a day. After a week do fifteen a day. A week later move to twenty a day and stay at twenty for the remainder of the program. Like any muscle, you have to continue with strengthening exercises to maintain the strength you've built.

As with any new exercise, get comfortable with the practices, but don't try to add too many at once. Ease into this one, as it can be a painful area to overwork.

Already doing PFMT exercises? Or do you want to be able to intensify the regimen once you get your twenty count a day down? Great! Here are some other exercises to try.

2. **PC Pump:** When you are more comfortable with the basic PC exercise, you can progress to a PC pump. As with the basic Kegel PC exercise, you will tighten the muscle with the in-breath, hold it for ten seconds, then bear down as you exhale. Practice for a few minutes each day. This is another hugely beneficial exercise for lovemaking, and great for vulva/vagina havers who would like to learn to ejaculate.

3. **PC Pullups:** Take a breath and relax your PC muscle. As you exhale, contract your PC muscle, pulling it upward. Repeat 9-18 times. Then contract your PC muscle for

ten seconds while breathing naturally. Repeat three times.

Here is One More Fun Exercise for Clitoris-Havers:

Squeeze your way to more pleasure exercise: Begin by washing your hands, and removing any rings or jewelry that may hinder your comfort. Get comfortable lying down or sitting at the edge of a chair. Insert two fingers inside your vagina. Squeeze your PC muscles around your fingers, then relax. Spread your fingers, keeping them relaxed but at a distance from each other. Take a breath, exhale and relax. Now contract your PC muscle again and see if you can bring your fingers together, holding the contraction for a count of ten. If not, don't worry, as it just takes practice. Repeat two more times with a ten-count hold.

Want to add weights? You may enjoy a product that allows you to lift weights outside of your body using your PC. Weights are available for all types of human genitalia.

Making Peace With Self-Pleasuring

Before we delve more deeply into a sex ed lesson on genitals that we should have all received but probably did not, let's discuss the importance of releasing any negative associations you may have with masturbation.

It is rare that humans don't pick up at least one negative association with masturbation. We are not often given permission to enjoy pleasure derived from our genitals. In fact, you may have some strong negative messages and/or stories to release. Letting go of these hindering messages will allow for so much freedom. If you have already made peace with masturbation and any negative associations you have with self-pleasuring, that is great!

Negative associations will only keep you from experiencing real satisfaction. It can also create issues in partnered sexual activities.

Let's begin with some assessment questions.

Bodily Pleasure Assessment:

- Where in your body do you usually feel non-sexual pleasure? What words would you use to describe the pleasurable sensations in your body?
- How are you currently connecting with pleasure that is non-sexual? How do those experiences leave you feeling? How have they contributed to your life?
- How has non-sexual touch with friends and loved ones felt?
- Have you enjoyed getting professional services that involve non-sexual touch, like getting your hair professionally washed, nails done, or massages?
- When you are in partnered relationships, how important is physical touch to you?
- Are you more comfortable giving or receiving pleasurable touch?
- Where in your body do you usually feel sexual pleasure? What words would you use to describe the pleasurable sensations in your body?

- Describe your associations with masturbation in three words?
- Were you given permission to touch your genitals?
- During partnered activities what level of comfort do you have with letting your partner stimulate your genitals?
- What is your level of comfort in touching your own genitals in front of a partner?
- How can you make peace with masturbation?

Getting to Know the Vagina and Vulva

Many of us are told as young children that we either have a vagina or a penis. Understandably then, many of us think of everything between a vagina-havers legs as being "the vagina". But the vagina is the internal part which cannot be seen. The vaginal canal is the avenue through which most humans are birthed into the world. Everything external is the vulva.

First, let's talk about the glorious vulva.

The Vulva

The vulva is the outer part of genitalia that is mostly visible. The vulva includes the labia, the clitoral glans and hood, the vaginal opening, and the urethra (through which you urinate).

The labia are the lips or folds of the vulva, which surrounds the vaginal opening. These lips go from the top of the pubic mound at the clitoris, down to the perineum below the vaginal opening.

That outer part that looks like sideways lips and has hair? That's the labia majora, which is often fleshier than the delicate (inner) labia minora. But for some humans with vulvas, the inner labia is larger than the outer labia. Vulvas, like all genitals, are like snowflakes and no two are alike.

Why are we not told that all genitals look different and are unique?

Labias come in a wide array of shapes, colors and sizes.

Unfortunately, many of the labias humans see online in pictures and videos have been altered to exemplify an ideal that seems to have been chosen for society.

Many labias seen online have been bleached, waxed, and surgically trimmed back in a procedure called "labiaplasty". Labiaplasty often leaves vulva-havers with reduced sensation and a lack of ability to experience pleasure. Trying to fit a societal ideal rarely works out well for humans. Embracing what we have and learning to appreciate our uniqueness leads to so much more pleasure.

Like hair found on other body parts, the hair that naturally grows on the labia majora and pubic mound is there as a protective barrier.

Personally, I have always hated the idea of shaving and have had a love/hate with waxing. On the one hand, I understand the desire to remove hair. The smooth feeling after a waxing can be super sensual, and let's be honest, having no hair can just be easier. But my body went through puberty already and feeling like it didn't is just weird to me. I want to feel like the adult vulva-having human that I am.

In the end, I decided to do what was best for my body. As it turns out, shaving and waxing off pubic hair isn't good for the vulva. Both shaving and waxing can cause nicks and cuts, irritations, and infections. Additionally, the lack of hair (your protective barrier), leaves the vulva/vagina more at risk of getting bacterial and viral infections, including STI's (Sexually Transmitted Infections). Keeping things groomed is healthier.

Let's move on to the Queen of Pleasure—the clitoris!

The clitoris is often thought of as the little nub above the urethra, but that is actually the glans clitoris, which is just the tip of the iceberg for this pleasure center. The whole clitoris is so much bigger! The clitoris has a shaft and crura (roots and legs) that extend internally along the pubic bone. As with all human body parts, the size of the clitoris varies from human-to-human, but clitorises can be up to 5 inches long.

Many magazine articles and books state that the human clitoris has an estimated 8,000 nerve endings. Unfortunately, this figure is based on a study done on a cow.

How many nerve endings does the human clitoris have? While this is yet unknown, medical professionals agree that the clitoris has many nerve endings. And, those nerves branch out to even more nerve endings. That means that vulva/vagina-havers can experience pleasure in many different ways!

Science is still researching to better understand how this pleasure network comes together. The clitoris has been left out of many medical books for a long time, and research on the clitoris is still relatively new.

One thing that is clear is that the clitoris's job is to provide pleasure.

Since the sizes and shapes of genitals vary greatly from human to human, it makes sense that how people like to be pleasured also varies. The most powerful vibration may be needed for one clit to be happy, while another may enjoy the lightest touch. Some clitoris-havers like direct stimulation of the clitoris, while others find it to be too sensitive. For others indirect contact along the sides of the clit may be preferred. This is where experimentation and lots of playtime really is your friend.

Now that you have gotten to know the vulva and clitoris better, let's meet the vagina.

The Vagina

If you are a vagina-haver then you know that the vagina is the part you bleed through, can birth a baby through, and may insert things into including for your personal pleasure.

Please note that the vagina is self-cleaning and does a very good job on its own. There is no need to use soaps, douches or other products inside the vagina, and doing so often alters the delicate balance within your vagina and can even lead to infections. Only the outer labia and pubic hair should be washed with soap. Also, make sure the vulva and pubic hair is fully dry before you get dressed. Vulvas and vaginas are not the biggest fans of being wet for prolonged periods of time (don't laze about in a wet swimsuit). Bacteria love to breed in moisture, and are not friends with your genitals. So dry off well. Vulvas and vaginas enjoy air, so sleeping naked or not wearing panties once in a while is not only just good sensual fun but can also keep your parts healthier.

There's a lot of debate in the gynecological world on whether or not the G-spot is, indeed, a thing. Some are adamant that it does exist; others insist it does not.

What we do know is that many humans with vaginas experience pleasure from stimulation of an area located about two inches inside the vagina often along the anterior (stomach-side) wall.

Researchers who first coined the term "G-spot" assert that it was never meant to be considered an actual "spot". They maintain that it was meant to be a research notation that a noticeable amount of clitoris-having humans were experiencing immense pleasure from stimulation of that particular area of the vagina.

Since the clitoral bulbs and crura contain erectile tissue (just like a penis) and swells with blood when aroused, that swelling enlarges clitoral tissue and can cause pressure against the anterior wall of the vaginal canal.

Personally, I love that pressure. I want fingers or a small glass toy rubbing that swollen feeling, because those are the orgasms that roll through my entire body and leave me smiling for days.

I am not alone. There is a good population of clitoris-having humans who experience a great deal of pleasure from stimulation of the G-spot area within their vaginas. We, in fact, have many counts of humans expressing that not only do they enjoy having that area stimulated, but that doing so can bring intense orgasms and sometimes ejaculation.

Ejaculation from the vagina is not yet fully understood.

What we do know is that behind the area where most people say their G-spot is located is the Skene's Glands, named after gynecologist Dr. Alexander Skene who wrote about them in 1880. When well-stimulated, the glands fill. This swelling can be physically felt in the vaginal wall if you are stimulating the G-spot area.

The Skene's glands produce an ejaculate substance, very similar to penis-haver's ejaculate, minus the sperm. It is a combination of lubrication, antimicrobial fluid, glucose and a prostatic enzyme called prostate specific antigen (PSA). PSA is the same fluid that the prostate produces.

Do not worry if you are a vagina-haver and you have not found a "spot" or bundle of nerves that brings you pleasure, or if you have not ejaculated. We are all different, and we all experience pleasure in different ways. Further exploration is going to reveal new pleasures that are specifically awesome for *you*.

Let's look at one last "spot" from which vagina-havers have reported experiencing intense pleasure.

At the back of the vagina is the cervix. The cervix is the lower part of the uterus that bulges into the top of the vagina. It feels round, rubbery or spongey. It can be very sensitive to the touch initially, despite having fewer nerve endings. This is especially true when it is getting bumped by a penis or dildo. But slowly building up with a gentle touch can lead to immense pleasure. Cervical orgasm can happen, my Love.

To the side, up under, and generally around the cervix is the A-spot. The A-spot, or anterior fornix, has the same debate around its existence as the G-spot. Many sex experts and women I have spoken with agree that incredible orgasms can be derived from stimulation of the A-spot.

The A-spot was coined by Dr. Chua Chee Ann of Malaysia. According to Dr. Chua Chee Ann, the A-spot is located above the cervix and can increase lubrication when stimulated, as well as provide some intense orgasms. It is also posited that the A-spot connects to the heart. After some profound A-spot experiences of my own, I wondered if there could be a vagus nerve connection. The vagus nerve runs from the brainstem down into the abdomen and its job is to tell the body to rest and destress, leading to improved mood and wellness.

I asked a leading sexual researcher and neurologist if the vagus nerve could possibly connect to the A-spot. He believed the possibility is definitely there. Only further research will allow us to know for sure, but if there is a vagus nerve connection to the A-spot area, it would mean that there is a *literal* heart connection. A vagus nerve connection could also explain the full-body orgasmic potential from having the A-spot stimulated. More to be revealed!

In the meantime, we can live in the mystery, enjoying the pleasure.

Explore for yourself and see.

The vagina and the vulva are powerhouses of pleasure.

Unfortunately, mainstream media and porn, both of which are used by many humans to understand sexuality, prioritizes penis-haver pleasure while rarely offering illustrations of the clitoris as the vulva-haver pleasure center. This is not helping to bridge the wide orgasmic gap between cis hetero penis-havers and vagina-having humans.

If you are unfamiliar with this orgasm or pleasure gap, let me share that 90-96% of cis hetero penis-having humans report climaxing every time they have penetrative sex, but only about 57% of cis hetero vagina-havers consistently (if ever) climax from these same experiences.

There are various reasons for this vast pleasure imbalance. Most cis vagina-havers are raised in a society that prioritizes penis-having humans and has made these penis-haver's pleasure the focal point of sexual relations. Sadly most humans receive limited (if any) sexual education, and even most medical books do not mention the clitoris. Pleasure for vulva/vagina havers has long been overlooked despite its importance, and the clitoris has been ignored as the epicenter of pleasure.

Studies have consistently shown that only 18% of vagina-havers can climax from penetration alone.

Why then is there so much focus on penetrative sex as *the* end-all-be-all avenue for sexual pleasure for all humans?

Education, exploration, and communication can solve all of this!

It is time for you vagina-havers to explore your own powerhouses.

In your uninterrupted space, take time to get to know your uniquely beautiful parts better. Perhaps you are already familiar with your genitals. Then take a moment to give some renewed love and appreciation to your precious parts.

Notice any negative feelings that arise with self-compassion. What societal programming has kept you from appreciating the vulva/vagina you have? Have you waxed, shaved or otherwise altered how your vulva appears? If so, how have those experiences left you feeling? What is most important is that these choices leave *you* feeling good.

Admire your uniqueness.

Really take your time. Does a slow super gentle touch stir some arousal? How does arousal change the shape, color and size of your vulva/vagina? Let yourself enjoy your own arousal - it is a beautiful, wondrous thing.

We often get into ruts about how we derive pleasure. Admiring your delicate folds may incite some new erogenous zones you didn't know you had. I still surprise myself with new ways to derive pleasure just by mixing up the way I touch myself. I would love for you to be surprised by new erotic self-discoveries.

Make sure to note any thoughts, feelings or epiphanies that arise for you. Don't forget to make note of any new pleasure revelations you have for future playtime, and to share with partners so they can please you.

Getting to Know the Penis

Like all human body parts, penises come in a wide array of unique sizes, shapes, and colors. Sensations and what feels best also vary from human to human. Today you penis-havers will be trying new ways to touch your penis, noticing what feels good.

Why am I having you explore genital pleasure? Because many humans try something that works and then stick with that method of masturbation. You have to try new things to discover new ways to enjoy your body. It is important to keep mixing it up.

Your body is capable of experiencing far more pleasure than you have tapped into, because we can always learn new ways to please ourselves. Are you multi-orgasmic yet? Once you become multi-orgasmic and can have full-body energy orgasms, you will have wellness tools that will serve you, no matter what life throws your way.

Let's get acquainted with the intimate anatomy of your pleasure center further.

The penis, testicles (testes) and prostate gland comprise most of the male genitalia. The penis is made of spongy tissue and contains no bones or muscles. It becomes erect when the spongy tissue fills with blood.

You penis-havers have probably already learned that washing the penis, testes, and pubic hair with soap and water helps keep them healthy. You surely have noticed that care should be taken not to get soap in the urethra. Have you learned the importance of letting your genital area dry fully to reduce bacterial growth, prevent sweating and therefore odors from occurring? Like the vulva/vagina, the penis isn't a fan of being wet for too long and is a big fan of air flow and staying dry.

Please do not spray colognes or other alcohol-based products on your genital area, which can be drying and lead to irritations that will make you uncomfortable. Do not use lotions, shampoos, conditioners on your genitals. Sugar products on the genitals can also lead to irritations and infections. A good quality natural lube is your friend. ;-)

Let's explore the penis some more.

There is a small tube that runs through the center of the penis called the urethra, which carries urine and semen out of the body. As one nears readiness to ejaculate semen, a valve shuts off the pathway of urine.

The head of the penis, called the glans, is very sensitive due to many nerve endings. Use this to your advantage, if you are not already doing so. Notice where your sweet spots are located.

In an uncircumcised penis the foreskin covers the glans when the penis is relaxed and pulls back to expose the glans when the penis is erect. Sadly, circumcision is reducing penis-haver pleasure, though there is little research to tell us by how much.

But there is a "spot" penis-havers might enjoy, and it is called the frenulum.

Just below the corona, or ring of tissue at the tip of the penis, is the frenulum. The frenulum has been likened to the clitoris and is often quite sensitive. Some humans may have a small bump to indicate the frenulum, while others do not. The flick of a tongue, finger, or small vibrating toy against the frenulum brings many penis-havers pleasure.

Let's move down to the testes, or "balls".

The two testicles (testes) are enclosed in skin called the scrotum. It is in the testes that sperm and male hormones are produced. A small tube, called the *vas deferens*, extends from each of the testes to the prostate gland. Semen is pushed through the urethra and out of the tip of the penis by contractions coming from the urethra and pelvic floor muscles, which is known as "ejaculation".

You may have noticed that the testes swell during sexual arousal and pull up tightly against the body. Pulling the testicles away from the body is one method of prolonging ejaculation (more on that later). Some humans with penises enjoy the sensation of having their testes licked, sucked, jiggled and played with, and even lightly tugged.

Where other pleasure centers might a penis-haver enjoy?

The prostate, which is a chestnut shaped gland at the center of the pelvis behind the pubic bone and just above the perineum, is often quite sensitive. Due to the high concentration of nerve endings in the anus, and its close proximity to the prostate gland, having the prostate stimulated can be very pleasurable. In fact, many humans with penises have reported that orgasms from the prostate can be intense and incredibly satisfying.

Enjoying the stimulation given through anal touch is normal, natural, and can be a healthy way to derive pleasure. There are many anal toys available, as well as toys specific to prostate play that may add to your pleasure. There are also guides available to assist prostate-havers with the how-to's of safe prostate massage, should you want to learn more.

It is helpful to remember that all human genitals fill with blood from front to back. That means that the penis gets blood flow first, so it takes longer for the prostate to become swollen and to have stimulation be pleasurable. It is important to be well aroused prior to prostate play, which can be done (carefully) through the perineum, anus, or both simultaneously. Always use lots of lube.

Ejaculation from the prostate is different from penile ejaculation in that it is usually flowing rather than in spurts and may produce more ejaculate. Like the G-spot versus clitoral orgasm, the prostate orgasm can be more intense and may result in an emotional response as well as a physical one. Simultaneous prostate and penile orgasms may result in a full-body orgasm.

Lastly, the perineum, the area between the testes and anus, is another area that might bring pleasure. Having the perineum stimulated is enjoyable for some humans. If you have not explored your own perineum area, today is a great time to explore it more.

How often do you make time to try new masturbation styles? Do you like to mix it up, or stick with your go-to for getting off?

Today's exercise will allow you to become more aware of your masturbation style.

We humans are prone to sticking with what works. This can create complications for a penis-haver in a few ways. First, you are limiting your potential, Friend. Also, your go-to way to bring yourself to climax could be messing up your game when you want to enjoy sexy time with a partner.

Think about the type of pressure and speed you use to climax. How replicable is that with your partner?

How often do you rely on pornographic materials to aid your process?

Type of grip, style of masturbation, speed at which you are rubbing it out, external visual stimulation usage, and the length of time it takes you to go from aroused to climax can all play a role in your partnered playtime. Know your habits and begin adding new types of ways to play into the mix.

It is time for your personal explorations to begin!

In a comfortable place where you will not be interrupted, get undressed and take some time to admire your penis and testes. You may want to use a hand mirror to see your testes, perineum, and anus more fully.

As you go about this journey, touch yourself in new and different ways. Go slowly, and explore as though you have never touched your penis before. Begin with a very light touch. Try using just the very tip of a finger to tease yourself. Slowly increase pressure and add fingers slowly. Beginning with one finger, to two, to three, and finally using a full grip.

Take your time touching and stroking the glans, or head of the penis. Add a drop of lube. Lightly run your lubed finger over the frenulum before stroking the shaft of your penis. How do the different sensations feel? Is it enjoyable, or does it feel frustrating not to just touch yourself as you usually do?

Play with the testes and perineum. If you already know that you enjoy anal play, combine it with stimulating your penis, noticing as arousal builds, then slowing things down.

You want to become more aware of the stages of your arousal and ejaculation. In the first phase the prostate contracts. These contractions are experienced as a pleasurable sensation or fluttering, which last for a few seconds. This is when the semen moves into the urethra. You may have a few drops of clear liquid drip out of the tip of your penis. You will want to prevent the next stage in which the semen is released through the penis.

Take your time, so you can test out how variations from the norm feel to you and noticing any new pleasure spots that could be explored more another time.

Below are two techniques to delay ejaculation that you may want to try.

Delaying Ejaculation for Humans With Penises:

The Pressure Point: There is a pressure point, known as the "Million Dollar Point", which can delay ejaculation and even prevent semen from spilling should you pass that point of no return. This technique for retention is called "Classic of the Immortal". Pressing on this point while contracting your PC muscle and inhaling deeply at the same time is one of the oldest techniques for ejaculation control.

The Million Dollar Point is located on the perineum, just in front of your anus. It may take some time to feel out the point, but you should be able to feel an indentation when you press on it.

Using the three middle fingers of your dominant hand, gently press up and feel for your urethral tube, which swells when you near ejaculation. You want to push on the urethral tube with your middle finger and press on each side of the urethral tube with the other two fingers. Contract your PC muscle. This may decrease your erection a little, but if you hit the right spot you will stop ejaculation from occurring. Breathing deeply and focusing your mind on pulling the sexual energy away from the genitals and toward your brain is also helpful. You may want to try using the breathing exercise below.

If you do put pressure on your urethral tube, it is important to massage the area later, contracting your PC a couple of times and circulating energy around in your body.

Scrotal Pulling: As I mentioned earlier, your testicles pull up toward your body just before ejaculation occurs. Using your thumb and forefinger, make a circle at the base of your penis, above the testicles, and pull down firmly to prevent ejaculation.

Please do not use pornography for these exercises. Being fully mentally present and in your body is an important part of increasing pleasure and sexual satisfaction.

Explore your perineum and Million Dollar Point. Can you feel the indentation with your fingers? You are going to continue to bring arousal, but prolong ejaculation for at least fifteen to twenty minutes. If you are used to ejaculating in a few minutes, this may be challenging. But maximizing pleasure, building your pleasure muscles and mastering new skills are worthwhile endeavors, Love.

Build arousal up and let it cool while maintaining a sense of desire.

Stay with these explorations, bringing yourself close, then using the breathing exercises, PC muscle and/or your pressure point to prevent ejaculation.

Press the tip of your tongue behind your teeth, breathe through your nose deeply and become still. Stabilize your breath. Lower arousal, but stay with desire. Keep your spine straight and tighten your PC muscle.

If necessary, press the index and middle finger of the left hand one inch over your right breast, which short circuits energy.

You might want to try exhaling and gnash your teeth together to produce more saliva, which naturally cools the body.

If you experience orgasm without ejaculating, congratulations, this is the beginning of multi-orgasmic potential. If not, don't be disappointed, as these things often take time and practice.

Keep training. Building pleasure muscles takes some work, but you will get there. Don't forget to make note of what worked for you.

CHAPTER FOUR

Abdomen - Where Emotions Lurk and Power Awaits

Humans use expressions like "feeling it in the gut" or a "gut reaction". Why is that? The abdomen is an emotional hub. This area of the body is also where personal power resides.

You have probably had experiences whereby an exchange with another human left you with uneasy feelings in your "gut". Another common experience is to feel energetically drained by others. Have you had your personal power usurped?

Personal energy is tied to our sense of purpose, our willpower, strength and identity. Another advantage to a lot of the practices in this playbook is that they will also serve to bring you greater awareness of yourself. Claiming one's power requires being aware of one's own energy and having boundaries to protect that energy.

Let's look more into personal energy.

Engaging Energy-Body Awareness

For the purpose of this playbook, and life in general, it is helpful to think of yourself as having an energy-body as well as a physical body. Perhaps you already have an awareness of your personal energy. Maybe you have a sensitivity to energy and the energy of those around you.

In chapter two we explored a couple of basic ways to lower and raise energy. We will be taking that groundwork and building upon it. What are you carrying in your energy? If you are not used to thinking of yourself as energy, I offer an energy awareness exercise below.

Notice thoughts and feelings that may arise as you work with your own energy-body, and be gentle with yourself. Energy work can release all kinds of stuff, so take that unnecessary energy to your compost pile so it can be mulched. Give yourself extra self-care, gentleness, and love through the work. Drinking extra water can also be helpful.

Energy Awareness Exercise:

Give yourself ten-to-fifteen uninterrupted minutes in your personal space for this exercise.

You may choose to do this exercise on either your bare arm or leg. Place your dominant hand on your other arm or on your thigh. Close your eyes. Feel the temperature of your hand against your skin. Feel the weight of your hand. Very slowly lift your hand away. Can you still feel a connection? How far away from your skin can you move your hand before you no longer feel that connection?

Very slowly move your hand parallel to your body bringing it nearer and farther away, sensing the energy field that extends around your body. Your energy-body can be measured. Can you feel it?

Start bringing more awareness to your energy throughout the next couple of days. This awareness is helpful in life, and will be very helpful to you for upcoming techniques, especially the sexual energy practices.

Caring for Your Energy-Body:

Let's talk more about the energy-body.

Stagnation of our life force can lead to diminished energy for going about our daily lives. Proper maintenance of our life force energy has been known to make a difference between feeling young and old, and why some may feel age more than others.

Just as unresolved emotions can get pushed down and "stuck" in our physical body, there can be a whole lot of undesirable energy hanging out in our energy-bodies.

When you really think about it, our energy-body is the real bridge between ourselves and the outside world. Energies we come in contact with as we go about being human can come home with us. Fortunately, we all have access to simple energetic cleansing exercises.

When we look at the history of humans, we see evidence that humans have long been using things like water and smoke to cleanse away unwanted energies.

Try the exercises below to cleanse and protect your energy-body.

Methods for Cleansing the Energy-Body: Many humans like to soak in water to cleanse their energetic-body. Salt water can provide a deeper cleanse. I have found that following a cleansing bath it can be particularly helpful to stay in the tub as the water drains, visualizing anything that needs to be cleansed from my energetic-body draining away. Swimming in flowing bodies of water, like the ocean, is another way that humans have cleansed their energy-bodies.

Humans have also long utilized smoke to cleanse energies away. Removing undesired energies by burning herbs (such as sage, cedar, and Palo Santo) is a practice that has been used at altars around the globe for many thousands of years.

The natural element of air in the form of wind can also be utilized to clear one's energy field. Standing in the wind, eyes closed, imaging all undesired energies being cleansed from the energy body can be a powerful practice.

Energetic boundary. Before you go out into the world, you can put up an energetic boundary. Some humans like to imagine an energetic bubble or light surrounding their body. I have always preferred visualizing something flowing around me, like water. I would encourage you to find imagery that suits you.

Making Altars for Deeper Connections

Building an altar is a wonderful way to set space and intention. You may find creating an altar to be a helpful way to hold space for your hopes and dreams and empower yourself.

Archeological evidence shows humans have long loved creating altars.

I would posit that we humans have a natural inclination towards altar-building, regardless of ideals. When I see a modern day desk, most humans choose to add items of meaning. Pictures of loved ones, places to be visited, or things desired. Often our innate desire for beauty is present. Whimsy is common, as it can lighten the stress. For example, action figures in someone's workspace may speak to their desire to have friends near or to partake in new adventures.

Historically, altars have been a way for humans to create a portal between themselves and their beloved Gods. But altars do not have to be tied with religion. Altars can be an anchor into desired manifestations, holding the intention, while also providing strength and comfort.

I love altar-building, and often create altars in each room of my house. A few items placed in a windowsill might remind me of being gentle with myself. A beautiful piece of carnelian sits with a candle on my desk to stir creativity. An ancestor altar honors those who have come before me and beloveds who left too soon, keeping them near and in my heart.

Take a look around your home and see where your altars may already be, or where a new one (or few) can go.

What can be put on an altar? Common items include candles, flowers, stones, shells, and other things from nature.

Incorporating the elements of fire, earth, air, water, and ether has been a longtime human practice. Having an intention and then intuitively choosing items that reflect those desires has worked best for me over the years. Which touchstones make you feel empowered? What's important is that the altar feels good and uplifts you and your overall space.

Happy altar-making!

Having Healthy Boundaries

It is healthy to set boundaries. Unfortunately boundary-setting is not often taught nor encouraged. Do you live in a people-pleasing society? Most of us do, and it can become pretty exhausting. This can be particularly true for vagina-having humans, who are often taught to please the world around them.

Having to make nice and appease others around one can lead to feelings of resentment and frustration. Having unrealistic expectations placed upon one can easily become energetically depleting.

Make no mistake, this is an offense to your personal power. Do not let yourself get physically, mentally and emotionally depleted by people-pleasing. You can be there for others and set limits.

It isn't always easy to say "no". Saying something simple like, "I wish I could but [insert reason, i.e. too tired, too much on my plate, it could compromise my health]" can soften your decline. Don't worry, boundary setting is like any other muscle, and it does get easier the more you do it. Fears of being viewed as a "bad human" or disappointing others in your life should not outweigh taking care of yourself.

Take baby steps towards having healthy boundaries with others. Be honest with yourself. Before taking on more than you have to give, check in with your own personal energy. Ask yourself if you have it in you. Assess why you might be trying to overgive.

Trust your instincts and value yourself and your wellbeing. Setting healthy boundaries is an integral self-love practice.

Moving, Rocking, and Claiming Your Power

You may already be happy about how your body gets its exercise. There may be room for improvement. Physical exercise can get monotonous. Life offers us humans a wide variety of exercises, mixing it up can be good for us. If you have been putting off adding needed physical movement, it's likely time to commit to your body.

Movement gets blood flowing, and keeps our organs, joints, muscles, and genitals healthy. Stamina and flexibility are incredibly advantageous on the sexy playground. We all know that living in a healthy body feels better, increases self-esteem, and can leave one feeling fabulous. Nothing like getting hips moving to stir up some pleasure.

If you are not currently giving your body the movement it requires, you could regret it, Friend. As I learned first-hand, lack of movement can make movement challenging. Your body is healthiest when it is kept active. If there is resistance, ask yourself why.

The body is made for movement. The body *wants* to move. If you are already experiencing challenges with your physical health, you are probably aware of the importance of implementing healthy forms of physical exercise into your life.

You may have experienced first-hand the wealth of stress-reducing benefits of physical movement.

Going for walks or hikes in nature was my favorite way to reduce mounting stress, while giving my body movement. I have never met a steep mountain I didn't want to climb. But when the steepness put undue pressure on my hips and knees, I ignored the twinges of pain I was starting to feel. Ignoring the body's messages is always a mistake. After years of many mountain climbs, the cartilage in my hip began to wear away, and more problematic symptoms appeared.

Please notice the messages your body is giving you. Again, there are tons of ways to move the body, and finding the ones that are truly supportive will serve you well.

It is also important to choose forms of physical movement that you enjoy. Make sure you balance that movement with beneficial stretching. The body likes to get cardio and flexibility training. Choose something that gets your heart going, then stretch things out. Stretching is undervalued. It is an excellent way to start your day. Maybe your body would enjoy stretches before you even get out of bed. Perhaps your body would love a few minutes of being stretched out during the day, and again at the end of the day.

Neglect can lead to having to do stretches with a physical therapist. Maybe it's better to implement some of these simple pleasures into your daily routine now? You won't regret it.

Want an outside-the-box method of stretching? Start with rocking your body, literally.

Rocking Your Body:

Consciously rocking my body has been beneficial to me as a way to stretch, ease tension, and make space in my body. Sometimes I rock to move energy and have huge full-body orgasms. Rocking can be used in a myriad of wonderful ways. I hope it becomes a valuable tool and pleasure for you, too.

Were you rocked when you were little? Rocking a child has been used by humans for a very long time. Rocking is soothing. Rocking is also incredibly beneficial in the bedroom.

Many of us humans sit on our booties for a lot of the day, which can lead to tightening of the hips, coccyx and lower back. Rocking helps loosen things up. It can help release stuck energies too, helping to make space in your body. It's also a wonderful way to ease tension and calm a stressed nervous system.

Have you ever heard the adage that "one is only as young as their spine is supple"? Having flexibility in your spine and pelvis can also be very beneficial for sexual pleasure. Everything that keeps the genitals getting good blood flow is aiding your sex life. Moving the pelvis is also necessary for moving sexual energy.

As always, tune in with yourself and take things to the compost pile as needed. We know that humans can hold stuck energies, emotions, and memories in the body. The pelvis is a common area for this "stuff" to reside. You may find yourself clearing space, or just enjoying some rockin' time.

For this exercise I would recommend sitting at the edge of a bed or couch. This could also be done in a chair. If you have a rocking chair, that's great, too. Ideally you will have some comfortable space behind you because I want you to have the freedom to move as needed.

You will be rocking your body, with a focus on your pelvis area.

Sit with your feet about shoulder width apart. Make sure both bare feet are flat on the floor. Engage your feet with the floor, noticing the feel of the floor.

Bring your awareness up into your knees. Then up to your hips. Feel your coccyx bone and your bottom against the surface you are sitting on.

Move your attention to your lower back. Take a breath and as you exhale pull your stomach in a little, rounding your tailbone as you do so.

Begin to rock gently back and forth a little bit. Keep your focus on your tailbone area. Increase the size of the movement slightly as well as the speed.

Now close your eyes. Continue rocking for a few minutes. Keep your body supported, but move intuitively in whatever way feels good to you, as long as you are using a rocking back-and-forth movement. Try to keep your focus on your pelvis area. Does your head naturally want to rock or bob up and down?

When you have completed the exercise, notice how you feel in your body.

How did rocking feel overall? What feelings came up? Was it pleasurable for you? Did it feel easy to move in your body? Did you feel as though they were areas that were stuck? If so, did rocking help relieve the stuck sensation?

Showing Up for Your Life's Moments

Your power is in the present moment. Being in your body in the moment is also the gateway for pleasurable experiences to happen. You are inviting enjoyment right here and now!

There are a bunch of buzzwords that get thrown around, and these terms can become annoying after a while. Notice any triggers to terminology used in this exercise (and throughout this book). It is important not to throw out the value of the message behind the terms. If you do find yourself triggered, take frustrations out in your compost pile, and soothe your system by getting out into Nature, throwing yourself a dance party, or whatever sounds like a fun, healthy way to release negative feelings for you.

For decades we have been told about the importance of presence.

Be in the "now".

Present moment awareness.

Mindfulness.

Let's be honest, most of us are so overwhelmed, overstimulated and overloaded by the mass quantities of information that we subject ourselves to each day, that the idea of presence can sound illusive. But bringing our awareness into the now is the remedy our body, minds, and spirits are craving.

All of the spiritual thought leaders recommend the use of present moment awareness practices to improve life experiences. But the concept preceded all of them. One of the most consistent spiritual teachings over the past thousands of years has been the importance of living mindfully as a cornerstone for having a happy and fulfilling life.

But many of us humans got too busy and distracted to hold onto the joy of the moment, and so the message grew. The more we didn't listen, the louder the message became. Now mindfulness practices are ubiquitous. UCLA and Harvard are not the only ones that have programs devoted to the study of using mindfulness practices. Most doctors, therapists, coaches, and trainers advocate for the use and importance of living with conscious presence.

Studies have shown that practicing mindfulness not only offers us a bevy of health and wellness benefits, the techniques increase our mental capabilities, motor skills, and decrease feelings of anxiety, stress and depression. By enacting present moment awareness we are likely to make better decisions, have better emotional control and make better connections with those around us. That presence can also increase our capacity for empathy and compassion.

Another gift of mindfulness is stepping into your own personal power. Lack of presence can lead to poor decision-making. It is much harder to get thrown off balance when you are living life fully in the moment. It's also far more difficult to be fooled, manipulated and otherwise have one's power taken away. Stay present, stay powerful.

There are many forms of mindfulness practices, many of which you will find in this playbook.

There is no skipping out on mindfulness because it is what we ALL need more of to combat the stressed out, info-rich society we have created for ourselves.

This is the soothing balm, Love. It is time to make a commitment to your presence.

The rewards include less stress, anxiety, worrying and loss of sleep. Without presence you miss out on enjoying the delicious and precious moments when they arrive. If you want true happiness and the ability to experience real satisfaction and fulfillment, you have to be able to show up here and now for it.

Is it easy? No, you live in a world competing for your presence! Mindfulness rewires your psychophysiology away from stress and towards better things. Bigger pleasure muscles = a happier life! You have already begun building. Be proud!

Bonus tip: I have found it immensely helpful to use a mantra to anchor me into the present moment. Saying something like, "Right here. Right now," a couple of times to myself quickly brings my focus back to the now. Maybe telling yourself, "Stay present," is the perfect reminder. I recommend finding your own anchors into present-moment awareness. What works to help you focus?

Harnessing and Appreciating Life's Micro-Moments of Pleasure

Marketing teams have been using the concept of micro-moments to guide you towards their agendas. Today you will begin to grab micro-moments of pleasure for *your* benefit, to de-stress, and to increase feelings of fulfillment. Yay!

This is such a simple way to implement the exercises you will find here. Because it is so doable, you stand a good chance of being able to implement more and more micro-moments into your life. This could be a technique that is a game changer for you. Or maybe it is not your thing. Just explore.

Being able to be in the moment and derive a feeling of real satisfaction from that moment translates beautifully on the bedroom playground. The more you wire your body and build up those pleasure muscles of yours, the greater your capacity for pleasure enhances. Yes!

Are you already familiar with the concept of micro-moments? Google created the idea to describe the times when we humans turn to our devices with an action in mind. Maybe you want to research something. Or you go online to buy something. These are considered "intent-rich moments". Marketers make and spend a lot of money to hijack and control these moments for their own goals and agendas.

Today, I would like for you to start thinking of how you can hijack moments of pleasure for your own wellbeing.

Life is busy. You are probably overwhelmed. I get it. Implementing a whole new technique into life can feel overwhelming. Our world was reporting epic levels of stress and anxiety before the pandemic, and it is no surprise that tension levels are on the rise even more now. That is why grabbing micro-moments are such a great way to decrease stress or anxiety that may creep in throughout your day. So doable, right? Indulging in micro-moments of pleasurable activities will be an easy way to implement techniques into your life.

As you journey through this playbook, challenge yourself to think in micro-moments.

When you next feel stress settle into your body at work, take a micro-moment to use one of the techniques you have learned.

There are many simple pleasures in this book that can be enjoyed in micro-moments.

Life is full of micro-moments that await your attention. A leisurely moment of stretching in the morning before you get out of bed. A micro-moment of greater enjoyment of your breakfast. A sensual moment in the shower. How can you find more micro-moments of pleasure today?

Experiencing Appreciation Through your Senses

An excellent way to amplify micro-moments of pleasure is by choosing a frame of mind that favors gratitude. Having a gratitude practice has been a popular wellness tool, touted by experts and researched and written about extensively. Studies consistently show that it can make a BIG difference in how we humans experience life.

Our human minds can get so wrapped up in what is wrong. Consciously looking at what is going right from a perspective of gratitude can quickly shift a person's mood and mind.

I propose that you merge the two practices - being in and enjoying the moment and experiencing a real sense of gratitude for the pleasure you're experiencing. This is what I mean by 'appreciation through the senses'.

If you can't enjoy simple things in life and be grateful for them, how are you going to delight in your body, and all of the pleasure you can experience?

This practice requires a tiny shift in mindset, if you are not already viewing life through a lens of appreciation. You know that adding simple pleasures can have profound effects. Adding in a scientifically proven gratitude practice is going to ensure that you get the most out of those pleasures. How cool is that?

What are three of your favorite new pleasure discoveries? The next time you experience them, I want you to really *feel* a sense of gratitude. Notice how you could welcome more of that sense of appreciation into your life.

Gratitude through the senses can easily become a daily practice. When you awaken to the profound potential of pleasures found in your everyday experiences, it can deeply enrich your life. Stimulating your senses begins by learning to pay attention in the present moment and then embodying a true sense of appreciation.

Connecting with Pleasure in Your Body

Pleasure is one of the best wellness tools we all have access to. Your body wants you to derive pleasure from it. Exploring new ways to do that is really fun!

Being in touch with what gives you pleasure and having the freedom to enjoy that satisfaction is another amazing way to claim one's personal power.

If you don't know your own body, you shut out potentials for experiencing pleasure. How do you know what you don't know? Our bodies are all different, and it is imperative to know what gives you enjoyment. The best way to do that is to keep exploring our own bodies. Then you will be able to show others how you like to be touched and pleased, which is an important part of a healthy and happy sex life.

Notice if feelings of resistance, shame, frustration, or other emotions begin to arise with this practice. Even with all of the great work you've done, don't be surprised if unresolved life stories around sexuality come into your mind. This release work can be a perpetual process because negative messages around sexuality and the body can be so deeply ingrained.

Are there messages or events from the past that want to be healed? Sexuality is complex, but you deserve to enjoy your sexuality and all of the pleasure your body can give you. Release what is getting in the way, so you can relax into your body and fully enjoy it.

There are so many silly reasons that we humans have gotten in the way of being able to enjoy our bodies. There have been many unhealthy and unsupportive stories and beliefs with which many of us were raised. Add to that mountains of myths and inaccurate information, and it is little wonder that so many humans feel discomfort and frustration around sexuality.

Unfortunately, many humans on our planet have experienced one or more sexual traumas. When trauma occurs, there can be a disconnect from the body as a way to cope or deal with the trauma. Healing *can* happen. Connecting with the body in non-sexual ways, opening back up to the experiences of pleasure in the body, while doing mindfulness practices in this playbook all help with healing and opening back up to pleasure.

Sexual pleasure is a natural way to reduce stress and anxiety while giving the body a burst of health benefits physically, physiologically, psychologically, and emotionally. Why do we not take better advantage of it? Anything that can strengthen the immune system, support heart and lung function, ease muscle cramps, reduce pain and boost brain power should be frequently turned to, utilized, and appreciated!

Oh, yes! We should definitely be grateful for the pleasure potentials of the body. Explore more ways your body gives you pleasure.

Exploring Your Erotic Pleasures

The longer I am in a body, the more I realize that there are always new ways to find pleasure in the body, and genital pleasure is only one area of the body through which this can be achieved.

I want you to explore your own body in ways that you might never have tried. Explore body parts from which you never imagined you could derive pleasure.

Pretend that you are your own new lover, exploring your body as though for the very first time. Relax. Enjoy. Take your time. There's no rush.

Please do not use external visual stimulation for this. That's right, no porn. Should you feel you need a little arousal encouragement, try reading some erotica. Erotica is a fantastic way to stir up desire, and it can enhance your visualization skills. Being able to use your imagination to get yourself hot and bothered is an incredible skill, especially for those humans that experience challenges around getting aroused or erect, or have difficulty reaching climax.

Set the mood in your personal space. Music, mood lighting, and scent all help.

Sitting or lying down, take a couple of breaths, and feel your body relax.

Sexual pleasure is a process that happens in the brain. Getting out of your head and stirring up desires in the mind are an important part of feeling aroused and being able to experience a satisfying climax.

Notice where your mind wants to go. Do you already have some sexy images playing in your head? Or are stories distracting from relaxing into a sexual mindset? Keep using breath to anchor you into the moment and naturally relax you.

What is your favorite fantasy? What scene from a movie, show, or video last got you super aroused? Let your mind go there for a minute.

Now, bring your attention back to your own body.

Using the lightest of touches, gently brush your hair back or softly run your hand across the top of your head. Let your fingertips softly caress your face, running them gently down the sides of your face, stroking your cheeks. Explore what feels good to you.

Use this same exploratory process all the way down your body. Move from your neck to your chest. Really take your time exploring from the outside of your breasts inward towards your nipples. Not all humans enjoy having their nipples touched. For many it can be a wonderful starting point after mental desires have been stirred. Does stimulating your nipples feel good? What if you barely tease just the tip of a hardened nipple? Notice color changes. Tease yourself.

You are welcome to keep fantasies playing, but not at the expense of being in your body. Use your mind as an aid to amplify pleasure, but don't let it distract you.

Try different levels of pressure. Touch, massage, knead, stroke, jiggle, pinch. Try everything.

You can also try adding lube to different body parts. Does lubrication on your nipples add to your arousal when you stimulate them?

Play with all of your body parts. Humans are able to experience pleasure and orgasms from stimulating unexpected body parts. It is only weird if you make it weird. And we let weird go, remember? So, relax and enjoy non-judgment.

Confession: I was shocked to learn that having my armpits licked felt unbelievably good and gave me orgasms. I thought, how? Answer: lots of nerves. Then I thought, "ewwww, that's gross". Just the fact that it gets so sweaty. Then I realized my upper lip and many other body parts sweat more. Why is educing pleasure from my armpits different from enjoyment derived from any other body part?

Explore it all, Love! Find your hot spots of blissful joy!

When you move explorations down to your genitals, try different positions. Use props, like pillows to change the positioning of your hips.

Does stimulating yourself while you are sitting, lying down, or standing feel different? If you always masturbate lying on your back try lying on your stomach and seeing what that feels like. I was surprised to find that climaxing from masturbating while standing up gave me a whole different type of orgasm.

What cool new ways to play can you discover?

We often get into ruts about how we derive pleasure. Admiring your delicate spots may incite some new erogenous zones you didn't know you had. I still surprise myself with new ways to derive pleasure just by mixing up the way I touch myself. I would love for you to be surprised by new erotic self-discoveries.

Shaking Your Hips and Booty

One of the most natural human dance inclinations is to shake one's booty. Moving the hips can help your body in a few ways, especially where pleasure is concerned. Many of us here in the Western world have lifestyles that don't support proper hip movement. A lot of us spend too much time sitting, which can put stress on the hips and low-back. So, should you have forgotten the connection to your hips, we will be saying 'hey' to them today. Booty shaking with intention allows you to shake out stuck emotion or clear cobwebs of stuck energy from long ago. Again, there is power in those hips, and you can reclaim your personal potency with movement.

Get yourself set up in your dance space. Do you have two upbeat, fun songs ready to play? Move intuitively, in whatever ways feel good to you. Starting with smaller movements allows the body to warm up and helps prevent injury. Begin just by feeling the floor against the soles of your feet. Circle your shoulders. Connect with your body. What wants to move? A wiggle, a bounce, some circles.

During the second song, I want you to put your focus on your hips and booty. Play with different patterns that can be made by the hips, being careful if you're not a frequent hip-roller. This is just an invitation. Unless you frequently shake it like you mean it, then go wild.

It is OK if feelings arise. Moving the body can bring about all kinds of emotions. Anger, sadness, joy, elation. There is no wrong or bad. Just be with whatever comes up. Write, compost and dance on.

After your booty-shaking dance jam, notice how you feel in your body. Is it craving more? Could your hips use more attention? Is dancing a pleasurable way to play in your body? If so, begin finding ways to incorporate dance moves into your everyday normal life. Perhaps you already do. Dance is a helpful practice for increasing pleasure in the body and for connecting with ourselves and partners. Or, potential partners.

Picking Out a New Toy

Ready to make a power play and explore what is possible? Sex toys are an excellent way to up your pleasure game. Buying yourself a pleasure device is an excellent way to empower yourself.

Any time you claim your pleasure you are also standing more strongly in your power. As you know, being able to invite more pleasure into your life is gold. Platinum? It is Amazing!

What associations do you have with sex toys? This is your opportunity to release false narrative around toys. If toys increase the pleasure you can experience in your body, why would you resist or push that away?

Our world has used sex toys for many thousands of years. Archaeologists have discovered all kinds of bone and stone dildos and other such pleasure devices.

While I can personally attest to the joys of a simple stone or glass dildo, I would be happy to shout from the rooftops about the new, more complex technology available to humans today. We are living in the Golden Age of sex and pleasure technology, Friend!

Unfortunately, human narratives around sex toys have not always been favorable.

The first time I purchased a sex toy, it was from an adult-only establishment in the "wrong part of town". My embarrassment combined with the societal shame I had been taught clung to me like a weighted coat. Head hung low, I quickly tried to take in the brightly colored plastic toys on display, most of them molded into phallic shapes.

My curiosity was outweighed by my urgent need to get the entire experience over with as quickly as possible. The man at the counter just eyed me occasionally, which was not a welcome invite to ask questions. It seemed doubtful he was qualified to assist my pleasure quest anyway. I grabbed a toy, hurriedly paid for it in cash and left the store with my new vibe wrapped tightly in a bag, which I tucked under my arm.

Fortunately, toy shopping has become far easier, and infinitely friendlier.

Do you already own sex toys? Great, you will be adding to your pleasure stash today. Perhaps you already have a new toy in mind.

I LOVE toys! Are you excited? I am excited for you!

For you first time shoppers, you are in for a treat. You have been exploring your body in new ways throughout this playbook, so knowing your body and what feels good to you will help guide you toward a toy that might be right for you.

As you will be using your toy with body parts made of delicate, permeable tissues, it is imperative that you buy a quality, non-toxic toy made of body safe materials. There are a lot of poor quality plastic toys out there, so it is up to you to pay attention to what you are purchasing. Look for toys that specify that they are made from "body safe" materials. Don't worry, finding a quality, safe toy does not have to be expensive.

A good quality simple vibrator can be a great starting point for all humans. Vibration can feel good all over the body, and can be a wonderful way to stimulate your senses before even touching your genital area.

Note to vagina-havers: unless you climax best from penetration, I would recommend that your first vibe toy not be phallic shaped.

Vibrators come in all shapes, sizes, and colors. Many vibes offer various speeds, strengths, and vibrational patterns. A handheld wand, or small palm-sized vibe often feels good to humans, and can be a wonderful starter toy.

For those humans with a penis, try using a vibe around your sensitive spots on and around the penis, along the perineum or anal area.

For those humans with clitorises, vibration toys may or may not feel awesome for you. Try using a toy along the edges of your vulva, and over the clitoral hood before going straight for the tip of your clit. You may want to wear underwear or clothing if the sensation feels too intense for you. Or, a larger plug-in vibrator may be needed for stronger vibration. Even if a wand toy does not work as a method of genital stimulation to allow you to reach orgasm, it often feels great as a legit body massager.

If you have concerns about vibration toys desensitizing your nether regions, rest easy. While strong vibration can temporarily overstimulate delicate nerves, they will not be permanently affected. Vibration toys also do not make it impossible to orgasm from other forms of stimulation. As with all methods to reach orgasm, it is best to mix it up.

My favorite toys are clitoral stimulators that use air pulse. There are also suction toys that are similar to air pulse, many of which aim to mimic oral sex. Some toys combine air and suction. All of these types of toys are relatively new technologies, and they are awesome! Says me, but also many other clitoris-having humans who have struggled with being able to orgasm. Many clitoris-having humans report that they are able to reach orgasm within minutes with this technology. If you are a vulva-haver and vibration doesn't allow you to experience climax, you may want to explore suction type toys.

If you have a penis, there are many types of toys for you, too - from a simple sleeve toy to more advanced toys. Many humans with penises get tempted to stick their penis into things they can find around the house. Please resist that temptation, which lands many humans in emergency rooms each year. Keep your penis safe and happy with a toy made especially for it.

If you find pleasure with anal stimulation, there are many toys available to aid you. Those with a prostate may enjoy prostate toys. It is important to use plenty of lube with anal and prostate play.

Have I inspired you to find a new toy? Do an online search and you will see that you can easily find many toys out there that will amplify your pleasure!

CHAPTER FIVE

Heart, Chest and Lungs - Expand Here for Immense Healing

How often do you think about the inner workings of your heart or lungs? The heart and lungs rarely get enough attention considering how very important they are for survival. When healthy, the heart keeps on beating, pumping blood through veins without any effort. The lungs also do their job of circulating vital-rich oxygen without a thought.

Making a connection with one's own heart may seem like an obscure concept, but science has shown that a heart-mind connection can be integral for our health and wellbeing. When we are in sync with our heart we can experience love, trust, peace and joy. But when things are out of balance with our heart, feelings of anger, resentment, possessiveness and mistrust can dominate our lives. Stress, anxiety and feelings of depression can all lead to severe heart issues. But there can also be a profound positive effect on heart health by using techniques like many detailed in this playbook.

Turning inward to the wisdom of your heart and lungs can allow opportunities for deep healing and transformation. Let's look more deeply at "heart intelligence", breathwork, and how to grow lasting connections with both.

Encouraging Self-compassion, Self-Acceptance, and Self-Love

We hear so much about the importance of self-love these days, but too few of us are able to experience it. It doesn't help that our world is filled with messages that speak to our inadequacies.

Does self-love feel like an elusive concept to you? Have you made efforts to find love for yourself, but you are still berating yourself when you feel inadequate or make a mistake? Most humans have a difficult time loving themselves.

Marketing teams bank on our lack of self-acceptance, which makes it easier to convince us that a product will fill that void. But we all know that no article of clothing, an electronic, or other shiny object is going to give us a genuine sense of love and satisfaction. It might be fun for a minute, but soon the empty feeling within returns.

Nothing outside ourselves will ever fill the inherent human need for love with which we were all born.

Becoming rich or famous will never fill that need.

The greatest "success" your mind can imagine will never fill that void within.

Only the love from your own heart can bring you the happiness you seek.

But how can you give yourself that love when a lifetime of societal programming has taught you to be hard on yourself and to seek your joy externally?

Self-criticism activates the same part of the brain as external stressors. When you mentally beat yourself up, your body experiences the physiological effects of stress from your self-judgments. As though life isn't stressful enough! Oof. We humans are so hard on ourselves.

Who has been the most compassionate, kind, loving voice in your life? It may be a family member, a good friend, or somebody else that has always mirrored true loving kindness for you. It is time to become that voice for yourself. Throughout this playbook, we delve more deeply into exercises to assist you with this process. Self-compassion is a great place to begin.

Adding a compassionate internal voice to soften any negative thinking that may arise within you is life-changing. When you can find love and acceptance for yourself through a compassionate lens, over and over again, your life and relationships will change in remarkable and beautiful ways. Life will always bring suffering. Suffering is part of the shared human condition. We should not be an additional cause for our own suffering.

Very few humans escape societal programming that has taught us to continually judge ourselves, make ourselves wrong, and beat ourselves up. It takes some work to find a truly compassionate self-view that allows for acceptance and the self-love we crave at our cores. Be gentle, explore with an open mind and heart. Every self-compassionate moment brings you closer.

Begin to notice when your mindset moves toward negative loops. Don't let yourself become over-identified with the messages. Instead compassionately see yourself through the lens of a friend in need. We all make mistakes. We all have places where we can learn and grow. Be supportive and encouraging rather than beating yourself up. Treat your beautiful deserving self as you would a best friend, small child, or other person to whom you are able to give open-heart loving kindness and patience.

Viewing your own mistakes or shortcomings with kindness will allow you to experience self-acceptance. The more we humans give ourselves acceptance, the more love enters on its own.

Self-love can be hard.

Self-compassion is the road to self-acceptance. The more you focus the lens of compassion upon yourself, the more you'll experience true self-acceptance. The more acceptance, the more you will grow the self-love you are seeking.

Every time you offer yourself kindness over your negative thoughts, you are expanding your heart space.

When you can see disappointments, suffering and other negative experiences in your life as a part of the collective human experience, without engaging with it, you can more easily experience self-acceptance.

What else commonly gets in the way of our self-acceptance? Our society's obsession with comparisons. Our world is filled with unrealistic ideals, and systems that urge us to want things that are just outside our grasp. Searching externally for validation can lead us to comparing our lives with those who have what we think we need in our lives. Comparing your life with another person's life is only going to make you feel less accepting and loving of yourself and your life. It is a no win, Friend.

We all have our own journeys to walk in our lifetime. Yet few of us give ourselves the freedom to feel good about doing our own thing. The moment you can stop comparing your life with others is the day you will experience the freedom you need to live the life you desire and deserve.

Making a Heart-Mind Connection

Being able to communicate with our hearts is an incredibly important skill for we humans to cultivate. Our heart has its own energy field and intelligence, as decades of science has shown.

Science used to believe that the heart just received messages from the brain, but now we understand that the heart sends even more messages *to* the brain.

Every time you experience stress or negative emotions, the heart's rhythmic pattern becomes erratic and disordered. These neural signals travel from the heart to the brain, which results in reinforcement of a stress response in the body, inhibiting brain function and leaving you less able to make effective decisions. That is why stress can lead one to acting out in impulsive and often unwise ways.

The heart-mind connection can also be used to your benefit as a way to reinforce positive emotional states, and keep you functioning at your best. Your heart is speaking to your brain whether you get involved or not. Better to orchestrate the conversation. Doing so will help guide you to the things that will truly nourish you.

If you have not made a heart connection yet, today you will begin that dialogue. You will never be able to make room for the truly meaningful things in your life if you are weighted down with protective armor and unable to hear your heart's wisdom. Be honest about how you have tuned out your heart. It is time for you to finally break free so you can experience all of the love and pleasure awaiting you!

Unfortunately, we live in a world where we can end up with scarring. Some dark and traumatic things occur. The desire to push these atrocities away is normal. These wounds hurt, so many humans have understandably built up armor over their hearts to protect themselves. But that protective shield also keeps out the good feelings, too.

Many humans turn towards substances to shield themselves from pain and negative feelings. Unhealthy shielding may allow for temporary numbing, but the feelings being pushed away are still there, dwelling inside. The more something is pushed away, the more likely it is to come up in inappropriate ways. That can get humans into all kinds of messes, can't it?

And there are additional problems with numbing. We humans were wired to feel, and numbing pain as a protective shield keeps all of the many opportunities life brings us to experience pleasure… just out of grasp.

How does that play out in daily life?

The food you eat doesn't bring real fulfillment. The wins and "successes" don't have the meaning they should. Even sex doesn't bring any lasting satisfaction. That is a HUGE red flag.

These disconnections lead to shallower living, and if a human no longer cares, then the shadows loom greater and chaos may even come out to play.

Have you ever found yourself in dangerous situations and you weren't even sure how you got there? Maybe warning signs got ignored. It happens to many humans. Humaning can be challenging and weird, right?

Fortunately, we humans can turn things around for ourselves. Sometimes deep healing can happen in an instant. Never underestimate your own ability to change your life.

Never underestimate the power of the heart as the ultimate healer it can be.

The work you have started here is already working its wondrous ways to speak to your heart, even if you were not consciously aware of it.

The exercise below will guide you towards opening an honest dialogue with your heart. Yes, it is time you two really talked. It has your best interest at heart. And your heart has its own intelligence and a measurable energy field. It speaks to your brain. Let's use that to your advantage to intentionally spread the messages of love, so any pain residing there can melt away.

The ability to give and receive love is paramount to life enjoyment. It begins with self-acceptance, which slowly becomes love for yourself. Once that self-love affair begins, the love and pleasure potential with others is boundless. You and I both know this is a game-changer for you, Friend. You have got this, because deep down inside you know you want to let go of the pain that got stuffed away in that beautiful heart of yours. You will feel so good afterwards. Once you begin living in accord with the heart, you become limitless. You will find yourself waking up excited to get up in the morning, smiling with satisfaction when you go to bed, and sleeping more peacefully at night.

It is time for your heart to return to its naturally calm, happy, healthy state. And then it can bring joys and pleasures into your life, the likes of which you have barely dreamed!

Show up, tune in, be honest about what is there and why, and be willing to release what you can. Sometimes it takes time to chip away at things, other times it is spontaneous. You are a warrior/ess just for trying. Opening a real and lasting dialogue with your heart can be scary. It can bring up all kinds of feelings. That is normal, natural, and healthy. You are doing the work. Be proud. Embrace this moment, and cherish it, for it's the real foundation for a life you love.

Conversing With the Heart:

Today you are going to have a conversation with your heart.

This is going to feel wonderful.

You are going to do this in your personal space. Make sure that you will not be distracted or interrupted.

Lie flat on your back, with any body parts supported as needed. Take a deep breath, and as you exhale release tension in your body. Take another breath and let the air fill your belly. As you exhale, release a little sigh. Take a third deep breath, enjoying the expansion in your belly all the way deep down to your pelvis. This time, as you exhale, allow yourself to organically make noise, releasing tension from your body.

Put your hands on your heart and shift your awareness to your heart area. Say 'hello" to your heart. Smile. Then relax your smile leaving the corners of your mouth turned upward a little bit.

Bring your awareness back to your heart.

Tell yourself, "I love you".

Think of something that you have done for which you feel very proud. Are you smiling? What does that sense of pride feel like in your body? Tell yourself how amazing you are.

As you do this exercise, continue to stay with whatever comes up for you emotionally. You are safe, and all is well. Anything that arises is likely old stuff that needs to be released. It is making way for better things in your life. So just let it roll through.

Allow the love from your own heart to wash through you. Your heart is there, beating whether you think about it or not. But it is also awaiting your attention, so it can guide you, help you, heal you.

Continue to use this exercise. Let your heart provide the love, wisdom, and guidance it was designed to give you.

Feeling the Love: Antonia's Rosewater Practice

One of my favorite self-love practices is a mirror exercise. I have had this little gem of a simple pleasure tucked away with me for many years, and it has served me well.

This practice might feel silly at first. That's OK. Just flow with it anyway. Sometimes these simple silly things can contribute to our lives in big ways.

This practice can be a subtle one, but it works. Showing up for and loving yourself makes space to love others. Self-love is required to trust in and receive other's love. The more you work with this practice, the more you'll increase self-love awareness, which contributes to every area of wellbeing in your life.

You will need a mirror, rose water, and some paper towels. The practice takes about 15 minutes.

I want you to do this at your personal bathroom mirror. Get your rosewater, a few sheets of paper towels, and your open heart. Remove any bathroom items that you have in front of your mirror that could get in the way.

Stand in front of the mirror and look at yourself. Smile at that beautiful being you see. Maybe say, "hello". If it feels stupid, just say whatever comes up for you. Maybe it's as simple as, "I don't know why Antonia is making me do this".

We are going to be cleansing the mirror using rosewater. As you do so I want you to really imagine putting loving energy into the mirror. You may want to picture the color pink, or whatever comes up for you. You are shining up that mirror to make it a lovefest area.

Look at your reflection again with the eyes of a best friend, mother, beloved, or whomever represents a loving figure in your mind.

Open your compassionate heart. Tell your reflection, "I love you".

Put your hand on your heart and shower the person you see before you with unconditional love. Look into your eyes with soft, loving eyes. Stay with it, noticing but not judging any feelings or emotions that might arise.

Give yourself time afterwards. You may find a need to express emotions. Give yourself space to process. What will support you? Write, paint, sing, walk in nature, laugh, cry, and be gentle with yourself. Compost as needed.

Keep up with this practice by greeting your reflection each morning with a verbal "I love you". It can be said silently to yourself in your head, but it can be even more potent to express your love verbally.

Whenever you feel like your mirror needs a little loving refresh, feel free to add a fresh layer of rosewater to shine it up. It smells nice, too.

Using Breath to De-stress and Heal

Breathwork is one of the best wellness tools for quickly taking the body from stressed to calm. Breathwork is a great way to quickly regain your calm. Being able to keep your cool as a human can be very helpful.

You already breathe all day, but by adding some focus you can tap into one of the best free techniques to de-stress available to you.

This is an easy tool for combating this crazy world the next time stress and anxiety creep in. Less anxiety, more relaxed. Ahhh… so simple.

Everyone from pro athletes to top executives, mystic yogis and modern-day biohackers use the power of breath. Some use breath to calm their bodies, focus their minds and lower their body's stress levels. Most conscious breath users appreciate breathwork because it helps them bring their A-game to activities.

A smaller group of humans use intensive controlled breathwork for purposes like clearing the body of trauma, allowing their bodies to tolerate extreme conditions, boosting the immune system, and to have transcendent experiences.

Controlled breathing exercises have been studied in controlled clinical settings for decades. Many experts have encouraged the use of breathing exercises to decrease feelings of stress and anxiety, restore a sense of peace and calmness in the body, increase awareness, and more. And breath is always just right there, waiting for you to consciously utilize it. How amazing is that?

Try to make breathwork a regular practice whenever feelings of overwhelm, anxiety, sadness or depression creep in. On the flip side, we will also be using breath to intensify your pleasure, so feel free to start playing with that on your own by breathing into your pleasure during solo or partnered sexy time.

Pro tip: Remember form.

Many of we humans slump. It is common to sit at computers or with phone in hand, rounded shoulders, caving in on our own lungs and diaphragms. Even relaxing on the couch we can find ourselves mindlessly slouched. And guess what? That's not a great way to get airflow into your lungs and bloodstream, where every cell in the body is waiting and wanting to be oxygenated.

That's why you have an incredible opportunity here. Because you will now be consciously adding mindful breathing exercises to your day, and you can also start correcting any tendencies you might have to slouch and restrict airflow.

Do you hold your breath when you are stressed? It is common. You have probably heard someone exclaim, "I'm so excited, I can hardly breathe!"

Do you ever get ridiculously busy? Of course you do. You are human. When you finally stop to take a break, have you ever said, "I just need to stop and breathe" or "I finally have time to take a breath!"

It feels good to use breathwork. Perhaps by reframing breathing as a simple pleasure your mind will remember to utilize the practices more.

When you do these exercises, really pay attention to how quickly a few consciously taken breaths can shift how you feel. Challenge yourself to start incorporating this invaluable tool more often.

Here are three awesomely simple controlled breathing exercises to begin:

4x4 Count Breath: Simply breathe in through the nose for four counts, then inhale and exhale in an equal four count measure. This rhythmic breath can be particularly calming, and a helpful way to soothe the nervous system. It can also be a useful aid in drifting off to sleep.

Elongated Exhale Breath: Inhale for three counts, exhale for more than three counts. Adjust the count to whatever feels most comfortable and soothing to you, as long as the exhale is longer than the inhale. This is particularly effective when stress is high because it quickly calms the nervous system.

* I am a fan of taking three deep breaths when I feel anxious or stressed. The elongated exhale exercise above, done in succession three times, is my top go-to de-stressor.

4X7X8 aka Relaxing Breath: Sit with your spine straight. Place the tip of your tongue on the area of the roof of your mouth against the back of your front teeth. You will be doing this breathing pattern four times, with tongue against teeth the entire time. Exhale completely through your mouth. Close your mouth and breath in through your nose for a count of four. Hold the breath for a count of seven. In one breath, exhale through the mouth for a count of eight. Inhale through the nose again, repeating this 4X7X8 breathing pattern three more times (for a total of four times.)

CHAPTER SIX

Throat - Communication Center and Bridge to the Outside World

The throat has important jobs, acting as both a hub for communication as well as a way to nourish the body. Our connection to our throats can affect how well we can articulate ourselves and how we can feed our bodies.

In its outward form, the throat gives us the gift of spoken word. Humans have touted the importance of the spoken word for many thousands of years. Beyond the ability to express, communicate and share with the outside world, our words can carry a deep emotional component with the power to help or hurt. When out of balance, there can be miscommunications, a tendency to interrupt or interject, and the need to under or over express oneself. When in balance, it is easy to express oneself with clarity, confidence and in ways that honor one's truth.

In its inward form, the throat allows us to taste (which helped humans know what was safe to eat) and sustain ourselves. Our world offers up a lot of opinions about how we should be feeding ourselves. I am of the mindset that only the individual should be making such choices for themselves.

Nourishing Up

We humans have made relationships with food overly complicated. I would never presume to tell you what foods are best for your body, as that is for you alone to decide. It can be helpful as humans to occasionally take a non-judgmental stock of the fuel one is putting into one's body.

Feeling good about the fuel you put into your body can make a pretty big difference to your sense of overall wellbeing. Having a healthy relationship with food can be a way to claim your own power.

Let's go back in time a bit.

Our ancestors were wired to use taste as a guide towards the foods that were healthiest for them. It is thought that this wiring prevents us humans from eating things that could poison or even kill us, or merely waste our time.

Today we enjoy wasting time with food. For some that can lead to unhealthy habits.

Another issue we run into is that, like other senses, our taste buds have often been hijacked. Now our guidance is often towards foods that are very flavorful but are usually less than healthy.

I am not here to lecture you on nutrition and eating. You know that eating right will keep you looking, feeling, and operating at your best. The human relationship with food has become incredibly complex. Emotions got involved. Working through dysfunctional relationships with food will free you.

Have you had a healthy relationship with food in your life? Maybe you have worked through specific challenges?

As with anything, how does it make you feel? Eating enough fresh fruits and vegetables tends to be good for humans, but if your body needs to survive in extreme conditions something high calorie and fatty may be more beneficial. We all have different nutritional needs, and only you can decide and know what keeps you operating at your healthiest.

Some questions in relation to food that can be helpful:

- Do you tend to eat as a way to nourish your body?
- How often do you use food as entertainment?
- Where have negative food associations caused challenges in your life?
- How does eating leave you feeling physically and emotionally?
- How often are you left feeling good about yourself and your nutritional choices after eating?
- Where could there be healing with your relationship to food? Do you have feelings of guilt or shame around food that need to be released?
- How could you improve your relationship with food so eating leaves you feeling good about yourself?

Use your compost pile to work through any thoughts, feelings, and insights as they arise.

Reclaiming and Re-Awakening Your Taste Buds

Now that you have done some fuel assessments, it is time to connect with your tastebud's truest desires. Have an open mind, a willingness to see if your taste buds have been hijacked, or if you are following their guidance.

Does any conversation around food trigger you? Or does the idea of playing with your mouth's delicate little sensors sound fun for you? Get ready for an oral awakening!

Many humans derive pleasure through their taste buds. There are a lot of little bitty sensors to use when it comes to our sense of taste. Much of the experience comes from our tongue and inside the mouth. But your sense of smell also plays an important role in taste.

As food got outsourced to other kitchens and company factories, competition led to trickery. How could human wiring be used to gain traction on sales? These days becoming a favorite household snack brand can be quite profitable.

How do you get humans hooked on a specific brand of tasty treats? Bring on bigger, bolder flavors. Crafting larger than life taste sensations in labs has worked wonders for sales. But at what cost to our taste buds and bodies?

None of this is any secret. We probably all know what a real life banana or grape tastes like. And we are also probably familiar with the brighter artificial versions. The more artificial flavor sensations that get ingested, the less likely one is to still derive pleasure from the real thing. Yet the natural variety is going to provide better nutrition and be healthier for the body.

Only you know what you put into your body and how much of it is the natural version or artificial variety. Since we are re-awakening senses, so you can enjoy all of the senses you have access to in that amazing body of yours, it would be helpful to take note of the present state of your taste buds.

If you make a habit of enjoying many processed foods, then your taste buds have probably been dulled out. If you use a lot of artificially scented beauty and household products, then you have likely diminished your sense of smell and taste. That's because petrochemicals in our environment can go into the nasal passages and even stick to the tongue.

It is possible to reclaim your sense of taste and get your taste buds back so you can enjoy real delights again. The body is amazing at resetting itself. Should you desire a reclamation of your sense of taste, begin with a cleanse. Get back to basics that are natural, like fruits, vegetables and unroasted and unsalted nuts and seeds. Free your palate up from artificial products, so your taste buds have time to regrow cells. Over time they will rebuild stronger and less damaged.

Take your time and enjoy your food. Slowing down is also going to ease digestion, which will make you more comfortable in your body, too.

Lastly, try to consciously create new associations for yourself around food. We can always come back and re-write the stories for ourselves. Many food companies have latched onto our childhood food associations, altered them, and sold them back to us through clever marketing campaigns. Interestingly, many food associations in marketing are tied to sexuality. Eat this and you will be soooo satisfied. How has that messaging looped into your mind's opinions on the foods you eat? As you examine where your taste buds may have been dulled, try to bring more awareness to any associations you may have, and how your wiring has been hijacked.

Throwing a Feast in your Honor

While food is here to nourish us, it can also be an incredible way to enjoy pleasure through the body. It is vital to your wellbeing to have positive associations and healthy pleasurable experiences with food.

The occasional and intentional enjoyment of decadences is good for the soul. This exercise will stir up your juices in many other yummy ways. If you are anything like me, creating a little personal feast is an inviting exercise. You deserve to derive pleasure from the foods you eat and having some special foods around will give you the chance to practice pleasure mindfulness through your taste buds. If any lingering doubts or objections arise, work through them at your compost pile.

The more senses you awaken and enjoy, the more it will awaken appreciation and enjoyment in every area of your life. Deriving pleasure orally can be one of the most erotic experiences, Friend.

There should be at least three foods in your kitchen you can turn to, indulge in and bring yourself smiles. For me, I need a cup of black tea with quality honey and a little cream in the morning. It makes me very happy. I love quality cheeses and breads or crackers. I also love to have a few fresh fruits around to nibble on that are pleasurable for me. Berries are wonderful. I also need some form of chocolate. I don't eat a lot of it, but a couple little pieces of chocolate occasionally makes me smile. Simple pleasures. What sounds fun to you?

Do you already enjoy simple pleasures through your taste buds? Excellent. What other flavors might delight you? This isn't about nutrition, per se. Maybe you feel nourished and delighted most by foods that are also healthy for you. That's great, but the goal is to treat yourself to foods that are pleasurable for you and leave you with a sense of having indulged in decadence.

Allow yourself at least three foods that you love. More is fine. This is supposed to be a feast, after all. Indulgence is welcome. You have been doing excellent work here, and you deserve a feast in your honor!

I would invite you to create a visually welcoming space for your 'feast'. Picnic on the living room floor with pillows and candlelight? Luxurious multi-course meal in the dining room? A simple celebration on the balcony, garden or patio under twinkle lights?

Try to include more of these simple food pleasures into your life. Giving yourself intentional indulgences often contributes to an overall sense of satisfaction and wellbeing. Savor the experience.

Speaking With Intention

Words can be easy to speak, but understanding the intention behind words requires some work. How often do you think about the words you speak? What about the words you use to describe yourself and your life? These verbal expressions are very telling.

Bringing awareness to the words we speak and recognizing the motivation or belief systems behind those words is transformative.

Start bringing more awareness to what you are verbally expressing. For one day, pay close attention to the words you choose and stories you tell. Make notes on paper or electronically to help you keep track of what you have been saying.

It can also be really helpful to notice when your throat becomes tight or constricted. When we over express the throat can become stressed, which can lead to coughing or soreness. When throat irritations occur, try to note what you were saying and to whom. Were you trying to communicate more than was necessary? Were you seeking validation? Was the person you were talking to worthy of your time and energy?

At the end of the day, notice which themes played out in the words and stories you expressed. Are you sharing positivity or negativity about yourself, your life, and others? Are your true beliefs and values being shared? How could you have a healthier communication style?

The more awareness you bring to what you are conveying to the outside world, the more you can shift towards healthy communications. Being in alignment with your expressions has profound effects on relationships with yourself, others and the world around you.

Exploring the Sounds of Your Pleasure

Pleasure can be reinforced and amplified through making sound. Are you familiar and comfortable with the noises you make when you experience various forms of pleasure? Laughter. A squeal of delight. Moaning, groaning, grunting, and screaming. Pleasure has many sounds; begin exploring your own noises.

You probably already make noises when you are pleased by certain simple pleasures - like the delight at seeing a loved one, when you are admiring the beauty of a sunset, or enjoying a favorite food.

Being comfortable with expressing pleasure enhances your ability to enjoy pleasure. It is also important that the noises you make are authentic for you. This exercise is designed as a check in on why you make the noises you do, if your sexy sounds feel genuine to you, and to allow you freedom to express yourself in the most beautiful and natural way possible.

Sounds allow for release. Sounds also amplify pleasure, and often the pleasure of your partner. Sound is a wave that can carry your pleasure to greater heights. Embrace it for the gift it can be.

We humans express our enjoyment of life's simple pleasures in a myriad of ways. We 'oh' and 'ah' over beautiful things.

We delight at pleasurable exchanges with loved ones and may even moan at the taste of delicious food. These noises contribute to your own physiological wellbeing because they soothe the nervous system while reinforcing the development of your pleasure muscles.

Freedom of self-expression can be challenging for humans, particularly when it is an expression of sexual enjoyment. The noises humans make when in the throes of ecstasy can often sound strange, and sometimes even scary, from intense, to joyful, and even macabre. There are no right or wrong noises, especially where the expression of pleasure is concerned. When we judge, we restrict our own pleasure. Time to liberate yourself from such hindrances, because your pleasure will no longer be denied.

Unfortunately, many humans have reported making noises during sex as a way to boost their partner's self-esteem, and/or to speed up a sexual encounter. Making fake pleasure sounds during sex is particularly common amongst cis heterosexual female-identified humans.

Studies find that a high percentage of cis hetero females have opted to make encouraging noises during unfulfilling sex to make their partners' feel good about themselves and/or to encourage their partners' climax to make the encounter end as quickly as possible.

Where are many humans learning to make sexy noises? Mostly it is learned from mainstream media and porn. It is not the porn industry's fault that most humans do not get proper sexual education and have to turn to online sources that may or may not guide them well. Porn unintentionally became one of the world's top resource for curious humans trying to figure out sex.

And I am not trying to make anyone feel wrong about having faked their climax. I have faked my pleasure. I didn't know better at the time, because, like many humans with a vulva/vagina, I was not taught that my pleasure is important. I was young, and while I knew how to climax when I was alone, I had no idea how to make that translate to enjoyment when I was partnered.

Our society does enough to shame us for our natural inclinations.

Making noise is a natural and healthy human expression.

It's time for you to make peace with noises you may have made that were not genuine and start embracing noises you authentically do make when you are truly experiencing pleasure in your body.

I want you to make noise because self expression is important and powerful. I want you to make pleasurable noises because sound amplifies pleasure in deep and profound ways. I want you to express yourself because you deserve to be heard, and expression of enjoyment can change your life in an instant.

Are you ready? Mmmmm.... Yesssssss!

Take at least ten minutes in a safe space where you will not be interrupted, nor overheard (if possible) and where you can feel comfortable and at ease with making noises. This may be your personal playground or someplace else. Notice without judgment any emotions, thoughts, beliefs, and messages that arise. Take your power back and reclaim your right to make noise and express yourself and your pleasure.

Get comfortable in the space where you are choosing to do this exercise. You may want to turn on a chill or upbeat song from one of your playlists. Making noise can be easier with background music. Sit or lie down. You may find it beneficial to do this practice with your eyes closed.

Take a couple of slow deep breaths and get more settled into your body. Imagine something that is pleasurable for you. This may be smelling your favorite flowers. It could be the last great meal or dessert you ate. Anything that gives you pleasure. What noise would that pleasure take? Express it now. How does that sound feel? Make another sound, feeling into it and maybe letting the noise you make get louder.

If it feels weird, start with a simple 'ohhhh' or 'ahhhh', or simply say the word 'yes'.

Sound can also be an excellent way to remove stuck emotions. If making noises suddenly carries you to places that feel like sadness, anger, or frustration, welcome the release. You are cracking things open so you can let go of what needs to go so there is room for the joy to be expressed.

What sounds resonate in your body and feel good to you?

Maybe this entire exercise just feels stupid. That's OK, too. What part of you is feeling that way, and is it your voice, or one that you heard growing up?

Laughter can be a great antidote for that. Laughter is great healing medicine.

You deserve to enjoy your life. You deserve to take up space. You deserve to be able to express yourself and your emotions — from the pain to the pleasure.

Making noise that is *just for you* is a powerful practice. As you continue with upcoming pleasures, consciously incorporate noises. You deserve to express yourself.

CHAPTER SEVEN

Head - Hub for Problems, Solutions and Experiences

The brain is both complex and clever, and a little dumb and hackable. Our minds are always trying to problem solve, but that can lead us into negative thinking spirals.

It is your responsibility to monitor your own thinking. Your mind does a great deal of perceiving and reasoning without effort on your part. The brain has an incredible way of operating on auto-pilot, running the same thinking patterns repetitively unless you step in and become the conscious pilot of your thoughts.

We also live in a world ever vying for our attention, filling our headspace with agendas that might not be our own.

When we are paying closer attention, we can shift and reprogram our thinking patterns.

Let's look more closely at what might be occupying your mind.

Assessing Your Distractions

Assessing what is pulling on your attention will help you streamline your life. Then you can intentionally add back things that nourish you and contribute to your energy levels. Won't that feel good?

We humans have created a world filled with distractions, many of which are draining us of feel-good hormones in a way that leaves us feeling depleted. Getting drained doesn't feel good, but making space for more pleasurable activities will. Space-clearing so you can have more playtime is an awesome endeavor.

Absence of presence keeps pleasure out of reach. Take back your pleasure, you will take back your life. But you have to make room for it.

Watch resistance that may arise. We humans can get pretty attached to our habits. Just take the plunge, get honest about what is really sucking on your attention, and be willing to take a break from it. You have so much to gain.

Sometimes we need to clear out the old to make room for new routines and habits. I have yet to meet a human who did not *actually* have time in their schedules to devote to their health and wellbeing. Yet, when I encourage people to implement some simple pleasure wellness tools into their lives, I am almost always met with, "Oh I don't have time for that".

But you don't get to argue for that limitation here.

We are going to be freeing up time in your schedule today! Hopefully on some level that feels like a relief.

Our world has been cleverly designed with all kinds of methods for grabbing your attention, distracting you away from accomplishing what you set out to do.

Our overstimulated systems can't help but fall into some rabbit holes, which may feel good in the moment, but rarely leave us with any real nourishment or sense of satisfaction. It is not our fault. The human brain kicks out the neurotransmitter dopamine as an incentive. This internal reward system used to lead us towards things that helped with our survival like food, sex, and preventing injury. But as our world became more complicated, our brains went from rewarding simple (intrinsic) pleasures like enjoying healthy berries or feeling aroused by a potential viable mate, to rewarding complex (extrinsic) rewards like working for a decent paycheck, swiping for matches on dating apps, and chasing 'likes' on social media.

Let's start with the giant among distractions: electronics. Most smartphones will tell you how often you are using them. But in an achiever society, lots of time spent on devices can be ascribed the deeply valued label of "productivity". In many societies lengthy hours spent on electronics may be viewed as a way to show how "devoted" a human can be. Rarely do these committed humans report experiencing a genuine sense of happiness and fulfillment from their devotion.

Time to rewire! Your health, peace of mind, and wellbeing is gained by mindfully taking stock of these distractions, then removing unnecessary time spent so you can fill that time with rewards that heal you and leave you feeling truly happy.

Streaming platforms are designed to distract for as long as possible, and our overstimulated minds find respite in binge-watching. Occasion binges can give us a way to get some much needed rest, but excessive binges won't nourish or strengthen our pleasure muscles.

Maybe you like to read lots of articles. Being informed is important, but overfilling our already full heads can become destructive when it compromises our health and wellbeing.

Is shopping for shiny things online a favored distraction for you? Perhaps you can get compulsive about online gaming. How much time does that consume? Does it contribute positively to your life? Anything done compulsively is a clue alerting us to an imbalance.

How many social media platforms do you use, and how often?

If you use multiple social media platforms, you are more prone to falling into an unconscious time suck. They are built for that. Try to pay extra attention to how much of your time goes where, including being honest about pitfalls.

Designers of major platforms readily admit that they designed their social media space to hijack your reward system. These platforms hijack attention with their little red indicator lights that cause your brain to release a quick fix of dopamine. So while having someone 'like' your new haircut photo may make you feel momentarily good and may give you a sense of validation, that reward won't release pent up stress and anxiety or leave you with any sustained satisfaction. It's actually just draining your dopamine reserves.

While many of us enjoy using platforms for their incredible ability to bridge miles, bringing us instant community and giving us that sense of belonging we humans crave, most of us fall prey to the dopamine loop time warp they were invented to be.

How often do you find yourself chasing that reward system?

"Did people 'like' my pic?"

"Who liked my pic?"

Refreshing feeds, chasing that reward.

I get it. I have fallen into the online traps plenty of times myself. Especially because I could validate my excessive time spent on social media for work. Have you lied to yourself in this way? Maybe, like me, you were building a brand, which is considered important in today's society. It can be so easy to justify things when it's "for work".

However, because most platforms have been brilliantly designed to keep us there longer than we usually intended, it can be easy for humans to open a program with one intention in mind, then find oneself having wasted away a chunk of time. Our original reason for being there becomes long forgotten. What was I doing again? Where did the time go? And why do I feel dissatisfied?

Studies show that not only do many social media platforms waste time, depleting our dopamine reserves, but our time there is leaving a lot of humans with feelings of inadequacy, a lowered sense of self-esteem, and increased feelings of stress, anxiety, and depression.

Seeking outside of ourselves never brings real fulfillment.

Comparing our lives with others will only bring us down. Why must we insist that life is a competition? A constant need for others' approval only adds to physiological stress.

Are you able to give yourself a sense of validation, or do you find yourself continually seeking validation externally?

When you have a life "win" or "success", does the achievement itself give you a true sense of satisfaction? Or do you continually find yourself needing and seeking outward validation for your victories to have any real meaning for you?

When you are on your deathbed looking back at your life, will you remember the 'likes' you got, or who watched your 'story'? How much of this one precious life will you have wanted to give to things that didn't add up to anything truly meaningful? Don't you think that you will care more about the moments you grabbed that had special meaning, like time with loved ones, and going after your heart's desires?

Today you are going to be reclaiming your mind, time, and self-esteem by assessing your online time usage.

Simply ask yourself the following **two questions**.

The **first question** is merely a notation of how much of your time was spent on electronics.

For every hour of your day today, make note of how much time you spent on your electronics that was not for work. I know that can be tricky in today's world. You have to be aware and honest to make this assessment accurate. Maybe you started out doing something for work then you got distracted by something and wasted ten minutes. I'm going to have you round up and count it as fifteen minutes. It will be easier to calculate electronics usage in fifteen minute increments for each hour. In the last hour did you spend no distracted time on electronics? Fifteen minutes? Thirty? Forty-five? Or did you end up in a rabbit hole for the whole hour? No judgments. Just the facts.

The **second question** you will ask yourself places a value for that time spent. For each of your hourly time increments spent online, ask yourself this question: What percentage of the time I just spent online brought value into my life?

On a scale of one to ten, one being the crappiest, most drained out you could feel from it, and ten being the most truly nourished and fulfilled you could feel, how did the time you spent on electronics make you feel?

This is for you, and there are no right or wrongs, just the freeing up of glorious new space to fill, so being conscious and bravely honest will benefit you.

At the end of the day add up your time increments.

Next add up your 1-10 values. Simply add the values you gave each hour then multiply it by the total number of hours you spent on electronics.

How much time did you spend on distractions today? What was the average value you felt you got out of that time?

Are you seeing some wasted time that could be freed up for more nourishing activities? It is time to create more space in your life, making way for better things.

As my gardening mom advises, prune rigorously. Time to be ruthless.

Bringing More Consciousness

Many of the practices in this playbook are designed to get you out of your head and into your body. It's helpful to assess how spending too much time in your head might be blocking you. Then take a few beautiful minutes to give that brain of yours a nice rest.

Being in your head probably comes naturally to you. Getting out of your head allows your nervous system to rest, which is going to feel awesome.

Many humans get in their own way by being in their heads too much. You may notice how being in your own head has an impact on sexual encounters and relationships. Hopefully you find pleasure in taking a few minutes to let your brain relax, reset, and rest. Just a few moments taken throughout the day can ease stress in remarkable ways. Being able to get out of your head is everything to life satisfaction.

With some genuine inner reflection, you can acknowledge where you most frequently let headspace dominate. When you admit what is going on in your head, you can shift it. This is not the time to shame, judge, or beat yourself up in any way. Greet yourself as a friend. Work through feelings that come up at your compost pile. Definitely take note of how it feels to actively take a break from thinking for a few minutes. Was it challenging, or did it feel like a welcome respite?

We humans have a tendency to overthink. This is especially true in societies that prioritize productivity and achievement while neglecting the need for down time.

I enjoy being in my head because I am ever researching, analyzing information, and writing. But I recognize that spending too much time in my head isn't healthy. Being in my head and ignoring my body was detrimental to my health. Now I know better. I am doing better. And it has made all the difference.

Overthinking is not healthy for any human. Our minds are so clever, always working to problem solve. The need to resolve matters can take our human minds into negative places if we spend too long musing. Research shows that the human mind left to wander on its own has a habit of leading us to negative thinking.

Negative thinking only adds to our feelings of stress and anxiety, compounding our inability to relax and enjoy life more often.

Have you noticed that when you spend time on things of the past it can lead to negative thinking that can leave you feeling regretful, sad, or frustrated? That is common. Too much energy focused on the past can lead to feelings of depression.

Perhaps your mind prefers to spend energy ruminating about the future. This often leads to negative thinking that can leave humans feeling anxious and worried.

Being in our heads is preventing us from enjoying life here and now in our bodies.

Overthinking is also the number one way humans hinder their sexual performance and ability to experience satisfaction. Let's look at some of the most common ways our overactive minds can get in our way in the bedroom. While mental loops could be endless, as all humans have their own unique stories playing out in their heads, there are a few commonly found shared stories.

Body image concerns is another common way humans get into their heads to decrease their pleasure potentials. Studies have found that this is particularly true for humans with vaginas, most commonly for cis females. Most humans with vaginas are raised in communities that teach them to "look pretty" and stresses the importance of being desirable for one's partner. Humans with penises can just as easily experience concerns about their bodies. Combined with the media and online inundation of unrealistic (and often unhealthy) body imagery, it is little wonder that we humans struggle with body image concerns - especially during already vulnerable sexual encounters.

What other ways can human's headspace wreck their pleasure game?

Letting your mind think too much! Thinking about work. Thinking about an upcoming meeting. Thinking about family. Thinking about an argument that you haven't let go. Thinking about what your partner might be thinking.

Pleasure is experienced in the moment, but many of us are not experiencing all of the wonderful pleasures that can be derived throughout the day because our attention is in our heads instead of our bodies.

Spend a little time assessing how your headspace could be in your way when it comes to enjoying life, including where sexuality is concerned. Be honest with yourself. This is just for you.

First, take the time you need for your assessment, and then at least three-to-five blissful minutes of uninterrupted time to get out of your head.

Here are some questions to assist with your assessment:

- How often do you find yourself trapped in the same negative mental loop?
- Are you prone to mentally beating yourself up? If so, about what, and how often?
- Are you able to mindfully take charge when your mind turns toward negative patterns or begins to wander?

- What stories are you telling yourself about your life? If you had to pick a couple of themes for your life story, what would they be?
- How much time do you spend reworking past experiences? How much of your mental energy goes to worrying about the future?
- When pleasuring yourself, how frequently does mind chatter get in the way of your ability to experience pleasure in your body?
- During partnered sexual activity do you find the stories in your head hinder your ability to be present? If so, what stories are you telling yourself, and how often?
- How would being able to consistently get out of your head and into your body contribute to increasing your pleasure potentials and overall life experience?

Breathing Out of Overthinking

Sitting or lying down, use a four-count inhale and exhale, breathing slowly in through the nose and out through the mouth. As you inhale, focus on the shape your breath makes as you inhale. Notice which parts of your body move from the expansion as you inhale. Give that expansion a shape, or an animal, or whatever your mind conceives. Just keep your focus on experiencing the inhalation and choose whatever shape you envision it taking. If this exercise is amusing or makes you smile, all the better. Keep with it for a few minutes, inhaling, naming a shape in your mind, then feeling the shape disappear as you exhale.

Was this exercise helpful in getting you out of your head for a moment? Stick with it. Getting out of headspace takes practice.

The more you turn inward and notice your thinking patterns as they are playing out in your head, the more you can prevent negative thinking pattern loops. It takes practice to become the observer of your own mind.

Pay more attention to your inner mental bully and try to compassionately cut off those critical or destructive thoughts when you notice them. We humans are far too hard on ourselves. It is time for you to liberate yourself and break those patterns. The more you make time to get out of your head and into your body the more you can decrease stress and anxiety while developing your capacity for experiencing more pleasure.

Singing Away Monkey Mind

Is your monkey mind driving you crazy? Try singing. Singing not only offers tons of health benefits, it is also one of the fastest, easiest ways to get out of your head. It can take your mood from pouty to carefree instantaneously, putting a smile on your face, or getting you laughing, which have similar wellness benefits. Being able to rapidly shift thinking away from negative thoughts is a ninja skill we should all acquire.

Creating New Memories with Scents

The use of scent for creating ambience and elevating desire in others has been around for tens of thousands of years. There have been a lot of musky floral playgrounds in our human history. If you have not already found your personal pleasurable scents, this is your invitation to.

Our connection to scent was wired in before we were born. Did you know that smells and emotions are stored as one memory?

Most of us create our lifetime associations with particular scents in our childhood. If you loved freshly mowed grass on a sunny day when roses were blooming, that memory is locked in as a happy, pleasurable experience for you.

The world around us is not naive to these associations, and they have been taking advantage of them for our whole lives.

Shopping is a scent fest designed just for us. We get pulled in by the wafts of freshly made coffee, cinnamon sticky buns, hot buttered popcorn.. Purchasing a new home is more inviting when there are smells of freshly baked cookies wafting from the kitchen. Studies consistently find that Western world penis-having humans tend to get aroused by the smell of pumpkin pie. Many humans are lured by lavender's dreaminess and relax around hints of eucalyptus. Even airlines have used scents to calm and ease passenger anxiety.

Scent is so powerful that companies hire olfactory branding experts to help create a bigger impression in our minds between their product and our precious childhood memories.

Since this is far from a new practice, companies have been creating bigger and bigger scent signatures to capture our attention.

Today that synthetic version found in a vanilla body lotion may smell better to your overstimulated nose than the scent of a quieter natural variety.

On and on it went, and our noses grew weary of the games and shut themselves down. These bigger scents can be overwhelming to the more sensitive of us.

Those accustomed to our artificially enhanced world may find it more challenging to appreciate the real deal now. Have you ever been around a smoker who couldn't smell the smoke all over their own clothes? Same concept. Just like many of our senses, our noses can get blown out. This is often the result of petroleum-based scents that are not at all good for our bodies.

Fortunately, you can improve your lost sense of smell. You have to let go of the artificial stuff you may be using. Laundry detergents, body wash, shampoo, hand soap. It's everywhere. With each move toward natural products, you are doing something wonderful for your senses.

Time to reclaim your nose. And reclaiming the use of scent for yourself. You will consciously wield the power of scent for your benefits. Maybe you already use scent as a way to ease your stress or to lift your spirits. That's great. If you don't have a favorite scent that elicits a sense of peace and another that makes you feel sexy, find them and bring those into your life.

Scent can be used as a form of consciously created space-setting. A well-chosen scent has the ability to instantly transform both a room and your mood. An inviting ambience is a fantastic antidote to stress that also works wonders to elevate one's pleasure. When you find favored scents, treasure those bottles.

Making intentional associations between scent and emotion is amazing. Especially when you are choosing personal power scents. Please choose two scents that appeal to you.

Find a calming scent that evokes a visceral relaxation response in your body. You may like lavender, jasmine, or sandalwood. You will know it is the right scent for you because you will (at least internally) say, "ahhhhh" when you smell it. The edges of your mouth might turn up in a little smile. Often the right calming scent makes you want to take a deep breath then release an exhale that eases body tension and makes you feel more relaxed. That's the one.

Then choose a sensual scent that stirs you. What does your sensual scent vibe smell like? Maybe a classic floral scent like rose, ylang ylang, cinnamon, or bergamot makes you feel sexy. I usually lean towards musky tropical florals carried in a light vanilla base. The magic is in the association for you. What wakes up your sensual side? That's what you want to add to your pleasure tool chest today.

Change up your signature scents as frequently as you desire. Notice but do not judge if your tastes change. Just roll with it, and feel free to mix things up if your internal guidance urges you to include a new scent in your life. The key is that the scents you choose should evoke good feelings for you.

Setting a Healthy Sleep Routine

We humans spend about a third of our lives sleeping. Unfortunately, many humans struggle with sleep issues at some point in their lives. Mind chatter is one of the most common culprits of sleep disturbances. Decreased sleep can not only leave us feeling drained, it can increase stress levels. Over time, poor sleep can increase chances of health issues.

When I was an undergraduate I completed a thesis correlating sleep deprivation with stress levels. It might seem obvious to any human who has endured a sustained lack of sleep that it becomes increasingly more difficult to function on reduced sleep, but there were few studies on the topic at the time. While my study was limited, I did find a significant correlation between sleep deprivation and increased stress levels.

What can one do to get the peaceful night's sleep we all desire?

Having a steady bedtime routine can be integral to getting a good night's rest. It also helps to have a bed and bedding that is comfortable and supports your body.

Humans are habitual creatures. A healthy bedtime routine tells the brain, "Okay, time to wind down. it's bedtime". What habits assist you with preparing your body and mind for sleep?

Light plays a role in the brain's natural melatonin-making process. I try to keep lights low in the evening, especially in the hour prior to my bedtime.

Electronics can keep the mind awake. You may already be aware of how helpful it is to decrease the light on your electronics at night. Be mindful that your content is soothing if you are using electronics before bed. Do you rest better after reading from a good book? Avoiding news stories and work emails before bed is often helpful.

Some people relax best after a warm or hot shower or bath. Should that be a part of your nightly routine?

Using many of the practices in this playbook can aid in a healthy sleep cycle.

Breathwork can be a wonderful tool to assist with peacefully falling asleep. I often turn to slow deep breaths to relax my body before drifting off to sleep.

There are many wonderful herbal remedies to assist one with falling asleep. Chamomile tea can be a soothing way to wind down that is also gentle on the stomach. Many humans are finding cannabidiol (CBD) and other cannabinoids to be helpful with anxiety and as a way to promote better sleep. Cannabinoids work with the endocannabinoid system (ECS). The ECS regulates many bodily systems, including sleep. What natural aids work for you?

Knowing your own best pre-bedtime habits and sticking with a routine can allow for the sleep you need to be your best. If mental activity is an obstacle to getting the rest you need, you may want to try meditating before bed.

Meditating Your Way Back to Yourself

Meditation is an excellent way to let go of old thinking, programming and garbage messing with your head, and wrecking havoc on your life and sexual game. Being able to get out of your head and into your body is gold in life and in the bedroom (or couch, or up against the wall, and all of the other fun places to play).

There are tons of ways to meditate and you will quickly reap the rewards. Your meditation benefits may include, but are in no way limited to: a quieter and more ordered mind, a soothed nervous system, bursts of insight and inspiration, improved communications, better sleep, an ability to observe and change old outdated thinking, decreased stress, lowered blood pressure, and so much more. Utilizing a form of meditation is a basic building block to a healthy, fulfilling life.

It has been estimated that 20-50 million humans around the globe meditate daily. Are you one of them? If you already have a meditation practice, then you get a free pass today. Go get your regularly scheduled internal journey on, and may it be exactly perfect for you.

Have you been avoiding a meditation practice, or just don't really feel like you need one? Uh, oh. It sounds like you haven't found the *right* practice for you. Today is the day you get to explore a way to implement a meditation practice that actually works for you. There are tons of ways to meditate!

You will need a practice you actually want to do each day, otherwise you won't want to stick with it.

And guess what. The vast majority of humans feel like a failure at meditation at the beginning, because we have been raised by a culture that values 'the mind' and outer achievements. Therefore, combating mind chatter is a huge obstacle for most of us. We just haven't been given the tools to get quiet and turn within. But being able to still the mind is an invaluable skill.

If you are starting fresh and needing to choose a practice, or if you are just ready for a change, I would encourage having a mindset that reassures you that it is impossible to fail at this. Did you hear that? For this exercise you get full credit just for showing up. That does not mean you are getting a free pass, though. You have to show up, pay attention, and keep with it, OK?

If after a week of trying a practice you aren't experiencing benefits from it, try a different meditation practice. It's like any exercise, you have to find what is enjoyable for you.

It took time for me to find a meditation practice I love and want to do each day. I would try sitting down to meditate each morning, be really into it for about a week or two, then I would just conveniently forget to make time for it. But when I found a method I enjoyed and actually wanted to sit down to do each morning, I found that the practice made a really big difference in my life. Honestly, it's one of the most worthwhile daily commitments to my health and wellbeing that I have made.

Let's look at some of the most common mediation practices.

Focused meditation: This is an incredibly common meditation practice, which involves concentrating on an internal (breath) or external source (a candle flame, counting with beads) to focus your attention. If you have a hard time focusing your attention, this may help you immensely, but it is likely to frustrate you in the beginning. Don't let your monkey mind make you feel like a meditation failure. Just keep showing up and paying attention, and after a week or so, if it still isn't feeling right, try a different form of mediation.

Mantra meditation: Maybe, like me, a mantra meditation will be a good practice for you. Even here, there are options and different paths. You might want to use a single word as your mantra. Or, perhaps you prefer a phrase. There are many Sanskrit mantras that have been used for centuries to focus the mind inward. Is it better to use a mantra out loud or just internally? Meditation experts usually recommend keeping the focus internal. But play around with what feels right and most helpful to you.

Mindfulness meditation: This practice has been used by Buddhists for centuries. In mindfulness meditation you become the silent observer, non-judgmentally witnessing your thoughts as they pass through your mind, letting them drift like clouds. This combines both concentration with awareness.

Movement meditation: Maybe you need to move your body to go within. Forms of movement mediation include: yoga, tai chi, or a walk down a path with deep awareness and concentration on a focal point, like breath, or the feel of your feet against the ground.

Guided meditation: There are many audio and video guided meditations available via apps on your phone, your favorite music source, and on many video platforms. A quick web search and your own intuition can probably help you find the perfect one for you.

Nature observance: At times the best method of meditation is to go outside, sit on the ground and focus your attention on your body touching the Earth and/or by silently observing nature around you. Notice the Earth beneath you, the temperature of the air, the feel of a breeze. If you pay attention to sounds, try not to focus on any one of them. Let yourself become more and more still. Ahhhh relax.

See, there's a meditation practice for everyone.

Choose one, and show up for it for at least one week. If it is making you unhappy after a week, choose a new method of meditation. Repeat until turning inward becomes a daily practice you enjoy and from which you are reaping benefits. The right meditation practice will bring welcome improvements into your life.

Massaging in New Joys

Another excellent tool for getting out of one's head and into the body is utilizing massage.

Do you massage your body? It's a natural human inclination to rub an area of the body when it hurts.

The skin is the largest organ of the body. It is also covered with sensors awaiting an experience like pleasure.

For the sake of this exercise you are not trying to build arousal. You will be giving yourself a non-sexual massage.

Self-massage feels wonderful and is an excellent way to check in with your body. Massage is one of the greatest free health and wellness tools we can instantly give to ourselves.

Ready to find some new joys? Take your favorite lotion or oil into your chill space. Massage usually feels better with lubrication.

Spend at least 15-20 minutes exploring what forms of touch make your body happy. More time may be better, so just listen to your own body wisdom.

Get undressed down to your underclothes or less, whichever is more comfortable for you. Sit or lie down with your oil or lotion.

As you make your way from the top of your head to the tips of your toes try using different strokes, speeds and pressures. Use your thumbs and fingers to work into places that may hold extra tension, or areas that feel particularly pleasurable to you.

Begin at the top of your head (or from toes to head, if preferred). Continue that way throughout your entire body. Approach your genitals in the same way you would any other body part you are massaging today. You are just paying attention to where there is tension, and what feels good to you.

Notice arousal, but do not chase it. For this exercise keep your focus on bringing awareness to the entire body.

Soothing the System with a Headrub

Massaging the scalp is a pleasurable sensation for most humans. It is also one of the fastest mood changing tools that improves circulation and has a wealth of physiological benefits that supports your nervous system and overall wellbeing. If you don't already rub your head for the sheer pleasure of it, you'll begin learning the art today. Then you can work that magic on your partner (or future partner).

Our society values living in our heads, and all that mental time can create a whole lot of built up tension. No wonder so many people live with daily headaches.

When something hurts, we as humans naturally tend to rub it. But when was the last time you really took the time to slowly stimulate your head with a focus on your pleasure?

The head has a lot of nerve endings to stimulate, which quickly calms the nervous system down. It's a fantastic way to shift from stress to yum almost instantly. But it can be a heavily overlooked wellness tool.

There are some lovely head rubbing tools out there, but today we will be relying on your fingertips to provide your noggin with sheer delight.

Where should you begin?

You may want to start at the temples, or hairline. Rubbing your temples in circles may be something you do already. Begin very lightly using the tips of your four fingers of both hands right at the hairline (or at the top of your forehead if you do not have hair on your head). Barely tease the hairline area with a light touch using the very tips of your fingers. Slowly increase pressure.

Then lovingly go exploring. You know what feels good to you. Try moving your fingertips in circles along the edges of your head. Use one hand to cradle the head, or carefully use a towel for support. Don't ignore the base of the skull, where tension can make muscles tight.

Notice if your neck wants attention too. Heads are heavy and you may find that stretching your neck becomes a part of your head rubbing. Take care of you.

Head rubs can also be used to bring energetic movement into the head. Perhaps a more vigorous head massage is what you need to get creative thoughts flowing and to help spark your next big idea.

Spend at least ten minutes on your head rub.

When you are done, give yourself a moment to just sit quietly, breathing slowly.

How does your head feel? Is your body more relaxed? Might this be a helpful tool to ease your mind and soothe your body?

"Thinking" Your Way to Orgasm

Studies have shown that we humans can "think" our way to orgasm. MRI scans confirmed this remarkable human ability. How humans accomplish this varies. Some study participants reported that they "thought" their way to orgasm by playing out fantasies in their minds. Others have used the ancient Tantric technique of moving sexual energy.

I personally began "thinking" my way to orgasm when personal interests in wellness led me to practices centered around moving sexual energy (as detailed below). What began as another exploration expanded my pleasure in ways I never would have imagined. Not only can I orgasm without physical touch, the pleasure is intense, deep and lasting. The orgasmic waves carry on and on, reaching far and wide throughout my body.

The human body is capable of so much pleasure. The ways through which we can experience pleasure abound.

Our ability to use mental skills to climax expands possibilities for everyone. I have found it to be both a pleasure builder and wellness tool. I hope it proves useful for you, too. Try using fantasy and visualization. Explore moving sexual energy. Mentally visualizing your own pleasure rewires your system towards experiencing more pleasure in your body. You're training or guiding your brain.

Mentally Moving Sexual Energy Exercise

Begin with the basic grounding exercise in chapter one. Getting grounded first will help you keep your balance, just as it does if you use it in the morning prior to going about your day or when life becomes extra stressful.

Once you feel grounded, lightly cup or touch your genitals until you can feel arousal stirring. Using a little mental fantasy for this is fine, but once you feel stirred bring your awareness more fully back into your body before proceeding.

Inhale and contract your PC muscle. As you exhale relax your PC muscle imagining your arousal building. Continue to inhale and exhale, experiencing the sexual energy building.

You can begin inviting your sexual energy to move by inhaling. Exhale, relaxing while mentally staying with the rising energy. Continue inhaling, while tightening your PC, and exhaling and relaxing while encouraging your sexual energy to move up your spine. Never force energy to move. It is always just an invitation.

Some find it helpful to breathe as though they were sipping through a straw, simultaneously imagining sipping the energy slowly up the spine. I prefer to breathe into the movement of the energy as it rises. Try different breathwork and use what works best for you.

You may want to rock your pelvis back and forth to encourage the energy to move upward from the base of your spine. It can also be helpful to let your chin bob up and down as you rock your pelvis. Can you feel the orgasmic energy move up your spine? It might feel like warmth, heat, or a slight tingling. More energy moving could create a pulsing, or spasming that is similar to orgasm in its contractions. It can take time to stir up movement, and that is totally OK. Don't be discouraged if it does not happen for you right away.

Keep breathing and moving energy. Continue with this practice for about five to ten minutes.

After you have become more accustomed to the practice of moving sexual energy, you may experience full-body orgasms. Maybe it happens the first time, or the hundredth. Just enjoy the journey.

Conclusion

We have covered a lot of ground here. Releasing societal and familial programming is a process, and the more you continue to implement these techniques and turn to the personal pleasures you've experienced here, the more benefits you will experience.

Paying attention to your body's messages will always serve you well. The more often you can bring present moment awareness to life, the easier it will become. You will better be able to enjoy the simple pleasures that abound in life. And little twinges of bodily discontent will go noticed, so you make adjustments to caregive your body's needs.

This playbook will always be here to guide. It was designed in a format that will allow you to reference specific areas in your life that could use some extra love and attention. Come back again and again as needed.

Keep utilizing and implementing the practices detailed here and continue exploring ways to de-stress and enjoy all the joys life brings your way.

It is time to say goodbye for now. May your continued explorations in pleasure become ever more fulfilling, and may that ripple out into your life in miraculous ways.

About the Author

Antonia Hall, M.A. is a transpersonal psychologist, health and wellness educator, and a frequent contributor for some of the world's top magazines including *Cosmopolitan, Women's Health, Reader's Digest,* and *O Oprah Magazine*. She is also frequently interviewed by media outlets like NBC News, The Today Show, Bravo TV, Buzzfeed, and Sirius XM. Antonia's work focuses on holistic health and wellness, self-empowerment, and removing inner barriers to allow for a more satisfying life. She is author of the award-winning book, *The Ultimate Guide to a Multi-Orgasmic Life*.

Learn more about Antonia and her work at antoniahall.com

www.ingramcontent.com/pod-product-compliance
Lightning Source LLC
Chambersburg PA
CBHW070427010526
44118CB00014B/1928